A THRIVING FOR EQUITY SERIES BOOK

Feel Better.
Do Better.

A GUIDE FOR PEOPLE WHO WANT TO CHANGE THE WORLD, BUT SOMETIMES HAVE TROUBLE MAKING IT TO LUNCH

DR. DEB SHINE VALENTINE

with Larissa Parson, Trevia Woods, Marquita Davis, David V. Valentine, Tamara Robinson, Kristen Mun, Jennifer Folayan, *and* Joyce Washington

Feel Better. Do Better. / Deborah Shine Valentine — 1st ed.

Paperback ISBN 9798986691602

Hardcover ISBN 9798986691619

CONTENTS

For Dave, Josh, and Devin. Oh my heart.

INTRODUCTION

To thrive — to grow or develop well, or vigorously;
to prosper, to flourish.[1]

Equity — the quality of being fair and impartial.
Equity is different from equality in that it recognizes each person
has different circumstances and needs, and therefore different
groups of people need different resources and opportunities allocated
to them in order to thrive.[2]

What is "fair" as it relates to equity isn't a question of what is the
same but rather the point from which a person begins.
Equity takes into account historical and other factors
in determining what is fair.[3]

There's a lot of talk these days about "thriving." I, for one, am all for it. I didn't become a life and leadership coach by accident. It was the result of my own desire to thrive, not just survive, as a human. And share what I discovered.

There's also a lot of talk about "equity," often linked with Diversity and Inclusion (DEI). Sometimes also "justice" (DEIJ or JEDI). I'm grateful for this also, very grateful. I suspect you are too. Though, like me, you may be discouraged by much of what you see as passing for DEIJ work — actions that look more like they are in support of the mandate, "Protect the institution of power from lawsuits by saying the right words and avoiding responsibility for ongoing systemic injustice or unconscious bias," than, "Let's notice and name where harm is happening, and make some changes around here!"

Maybe you're reading this book because you've been in this fight for decades. You've dedicated your life to being the change you want to see in the world. And you're tired. Really tired.

Maybe you're relatively new in your commitment to taking action to make the world a place in which all bodies get the same chance to survive and thrive. You've had blinders on your whole life, and now that you see what's going on, you feel a sense of urgency to make things better. But you don't know how.

In either case, my hunch is you don't just *see* the oppression and suffering that surrounds you; you *feel* it. Deeply. In your heart, in your bones, in every cell of your body.

You want to change the world, but sometimes you have trouble just making it to lunch. It's all… Just. So. Hard.

Maybe the suffering hits you particularly hard and deep because it's *your* pain and the pain of your people. You've lived it. You *are* living it.

Maybe it hits hard because you can see how you and your people have *caused* incredible suffering for others and continue to do so. Perhaps both of these realities live inside your body and your lineage.

I see you.

You're working so hard to do the right thing — or to figure out what the right thing is and how you can make yourself do it.

You acknowledge your privileges (race, class, gender, ability, sexual orientation, religion, etc.), and you feel more than a little uncomfortable about them, at least some of the time. But you aren't sure what to do with that discomfort other than to feel bad and try harder.

Your joy-to-justice ratio is out of whack.

Maybe you're working for justice, but there's not much joy in it. Or you're stuck in freeze mode, finding neither joy nor justice.

I've been there.

The idea of "thriving for equity" emerged out of my own complete failure to suffer enough to make the world a better place. And my desperate need to find a way to enjoy life enough to want to keep waking up in the morning.

My failure to be able to follow the path of "downward mobility" and self-sacrifice in order to do the work I felt called to do in the world took me on quite the journey.

I went to church a lot and was a dedicated member of my religious community. I read almost every self-help book I could find. After getting a Ph.D. and a tenure-track professorship, I swallowed my pride and hired (and then became) a life coach. I explored a variety of alternative health, wellness, and spiritual paths to find healing for my heart, soul, and body.

It helped. I started to make a bit of progress towards my own thriving.

But there was still a problem. I found very little discussion of racism, classism, transphobia, or ableism in the healing communities where I spent more and more of my time. More often than not, the (mostly White, cisgender, able-bodied) people I met in these circles — with whom, I might add, I share many of my privileged identities — were adamantly resistant and defensive if conversations about racism arose, which they rarely did.

Mostly there was just silence, often with a side of cultural appropriation, as spiritual practices from Indigenous and Eastern cultures were brought in to help those of us who were starving for new ways to feed our European and American souls.

I started wondering if there might be another way. A way that integrated the path of seeking to thrive as an individual human and the path of seeking to build a more equitable and just world. Spoiler alert. There is.

I'm far from being the only one on this path — and White people aren't the only ones who need it. Nor are we leading the way. In fact, people like adrienne maree brown — a seasoned social activist, a queer Black woman, and author of the book *Pleasure Activism* (among others) — and Dr. Amanda Kemp — artist, activist, and founder of Racial Justice from the Heart — are well down that path and leading many others. Also, lots of young people are creating businesses with flexible hours, prioritizing fair pay and full-consent sales practices over massive profit margins — and refusing to work for organizations whose values don't align with theirs.

But there's still a pretty intense cancel culture in the social justice world — a culture of naming and shaming people for not doing enough or saying the wrong thing and dismissing people as shallow when they express a desire to be paid a living wage.

The non-profit world still tends to be a place where instead of getting bound by the golden handcuffs of the corporate world, it's the guilt-en handcuffs of, "But surely you won't turn away from children (or the poor, or the imprisoned, or the Earth, or _____)," that lock us into lifestyles of sacrifice and suffering. These shame-filled "shoulds" harm our bodies, our relationships, and make lives filled with play and joy seem like childhood fantasies.

The guilt-en cuffs work well on artists and other creatives too. And on moms. There's a special line of guilt-en handcuffs for moms.

From my perspective, far too many of us still believe that to do good, we must suffer. We believe to make up for our sins or the sins of our ancestors; we must suffer. We believe to be good moms/artists/teachers; we must suffer. We believe to make up for our privileges; we must suffer.

We buy into the belief that our misery is an essential component of our work in the world.

Well, the suffering, striving, and just surviving path to changing the world for the better didn't work for me. And I'm guessing it's not working for you either.

I — and the incredible BIPOC colleagues who have contributed to this book — will go so far as to say it's not working for the world or for those dear ones you want to help.

We believe there is another way. I call it Thriving for Equity. This book is a guide for those of you who want to try it on for size.

Take the parts that fit. Toss what doesn't.

Then step out into the world so turned-on by all of it that you radiate the love, healing, and hope that you long for. That's what will change the world. You, in all of your courageous, joyful glory, stepping out and connecting with other amazing human beings who want to live from some new paradigms.

You CAN feel better, AND you can do better.

Here's to you and all of us, Thriving for Equity,

Deb

Financial Transparency Statement

The primary purpose of this book, and my business, Thriving for Equity, is to join others across the world to infuse more love, healing, pleasure, and joy into our work to dismantle systems of oppression that hurt all living beings, including the Earth herself.

The second purpose of this book is to make my work and the work of the contributors accessible to people who can't work directly with us. I, for example, know that my personalized coaching packages are well out of the range of possibility for many people. Though it is part of my business model to offer discounted pricing for some of those packages, it's still a very small number of people that I can serve that way. This book offers access to key components of the work I do with 1:1 clients at a much lower price point.

My business is not a non-profit. The proceeds from this book (and profits, if there are any) will nourish and nurture my coaching and consulting business and the businesses of the contributors. We want to be transparent about the fact that a purpose of our investment in this book is to share our work with a broader audience. That means it is a marketing tool for us.

Marketing gets a bad rap because it is often coercive and dishonest. But that's not how we roll. We all believe in full consent. None of us use pushy sales tactics. We all want people who work with us to feel a full body and heart, "Yes!" to whatever investment they make to do so. We hope that some readers also end up being clients. That would be delightful. And if you, dear reader, are happy with the book and go on to live a life that is better because of it. That is also delightful!

Initial proceeds from book sales will go towards covering the costs of getting this book out into the world, which include small payments (in cash or books) to each of the contributors for their time and investment in this project, payments to the company that helped me produce it, the cost of my assistant's time supporting it, and costs of ongoing marketing. When there are actual profits, each contributor will receive a portion of those profits based on the percentage of their contribution to the book.

If, having read this statement, you feel uncomfortable investing in the cost of the book or are genuinely unable to do so, please email me at debshine@thriving4equity.com to request a refund or a free copy.

Side note, in case you're interested in why I chose not to go the non-profit route:

The non-profit world is closely tied to the for-profit world and people who have benefitted the most from capitalism. That's not inherently bad, but it can lead to the funding and de-funding of projects based on the desires and whims of the most powerful. It can lead to hours of unpaid labor writing grants, meeting with wealthy philanthropists, and reporting back to funders. There's a lot of governmental control and bureaucratic hoops to jump through. I may have a non-profit arm to my work at some point, but right now, it feels better to me to create services and products that are of such beautiful service to people that they love exchanging money for them. And then fund low or no-cost options myself through the profits. Also, as a woman who worked for decades in the field of Early Childhood Education, a predominantly female field that has been atrociously undervalued, it has been important to my individual journey with internalized sexism to get to a place where I could choose to value my time and expertise, and that of those I work with, in ways that challenge that history.

PART 1

FEEL BETTER

There's a reason that you picked up this book. I'm not sure what yours is exactly, but I have a hunch that you're running on empty in some way. That's why we're starting with a focus on some changes you can make that will help you start to feel nourished in heart, mind, body, and spirit. These chapters are genuine invitations, not obligations.

You get to say, "Yes," or, "No," or, "No Thanks," or, "Not Now," to these invitations.

My hope is that you find that many of them feel like water raining gently on hot, dry, parched land and delicious, nourishing soup on a cold winter day somehow magically combined.

My hope is that they will help you to honor yourself, your body, and your heart. Because I believe that you deserve a depth of love and care that only you can give to yourself. You deserve it because you are created and already loved by the force that creates — Love, God/dess, the Universe, Nature, whatever you call it.

I believe you can give this love to yourself because you have that spark of Love in you.

I could be wrong about the nature of things. And you don't have to believe in any kind of force bigger than you to find this book useful.

But you will need to uplevel your love for the Amazing One that YOU are if you want to feel better.

And when you do, the whole world will start to sparkle with Beauty and Possibility.

Intrigued? Come with me. I have some invitations for you.

YOUR SUFFERING AND EXHAUSTION DON'T HELP ANY CAUSE EXCEPT THE CAUSE OF PATRIARCHY, WHITE SUPREMACY, AND CAPITALISM — EVEN IF YOU ARE WHITE, EVEN IF YOU ARE MALE, AND ESPECIALLY IF YOU ARE NEITHER WHITE NOR MALE

THIS IS AN INVITATION TO LET THEM GO

I did a survey once asking people in my community what children's books currently represented their lives. One of the options was *The Giving Tree* by Shel Silverstein. It's a bestseller. And I hate it. I really do. I'm not going to apologize for saying so.

The book is about the relationship between a tree and a White guy. It follows the guy's whole life with the tree, from boyhood to old age, during which the tree just keeps giving and giving and giving until, in the end, it's just a stump. And the old guy sits on it.

Can I say that way too many people in my (admittedly very small) survey identified with being the stump? More specifically way too many women. And I'd wager good money on a bet that if we did the survey with a group of social justice activists, there would be a lot of stumps. BIPOC or queer social activists specifically? Probably even more. Moms? Double that bet.

There would be some White guy stumps too. I've coached them. They'd be the guys who have come to recognize that they pretty much have all the privileges, and they figure the only way to bring balance back to the equation is to give like the tree — until there's virtually nothing left.

So, they do. And we do. Give and give and sacrifice our own health and joy and well-being in the hopes that our sacrifice is bringing life to someone else. Or that it will eventually. Or that at least we are "doing what's right" and not being one of those selfish, self-centered people who are destroying the world.

And there *are* a number of those. And the imbalance of wealth and resources in our world right now *is* causing harm. But that doesn't mean that choosing to cause your own suffering is going to help.

Your failure and poverty (whether that is spiritual, financial, physical, emotional, relational, or otherwise) don't help dismantle systems of oppression.

But living as your most vital, alive, loving, empowered self could.

And when I say "empowered," I don't mean the messed up hierarchical version of power that exercises power OVER others, that takes more than it gives, speaks more than it listens. I mean *empowered* to be the essence of who you are. Whatever you call that part — your True Self, your Inner Wisdom. Your Soul.

Just like any other living being. Just like the earth. Just like trees. Just like children. That part needs to be nourished and loved to flourish.

And when you do — when you flourish — it is an affront to the systems of oppression that tell us that there isn't enough for all of us. It's a challenge to the belief that some people are worthy of more respect than others. It's an invitation to let go of systems that treat some bodies as less valuable than others and moral codes in which virtual perfection is required before love and compassion can be received.

The challenge that your flourishing presents to systems of oppression is particularly powerful if you hold many of the identities that these systems have degraded — if you live in a Black body, a woman's body, a non-gender-conforming body, a disabled body.

And if you hold many identities of privilege? If you are (God forbid!) a White, cisgender, Christian, heterosexual, upper-class guy, for example? Or a highly educated, middle-class, White woman like me? How could your thriving help dismantle systems of oppression?

Well, I ask you, how effective have you been so far — working on the edge of burnout, depressed, anxious, angry, and over-whelmed?

There's your answer.

I don't know about you, but I've never been able to suffer enough to make someone else feel better. Not really. Not over the long haul.

Julia Cameron, author of *The Artist's Way*, says that often when we don't give ourselves what we need, we become, "vexed, angry, out-of-sorts...sullen, depressed, hostile...like cornered animals snarling at our family and friends to leave us alone and stop making unreasonable demands," when, in fact, "we are the ones making unreasonable demands" (p.96-97).[1]

The truth is you need what you need, and wishing you didn't doesn't make it go away. A car needs gas to run. Really fancy/sensitive cars often need really fancy and expensive gas. We don't expect them to run without what they need. That would be UNREASONABLE. We expect that they will break down if we don't give them what they need. Same with plants. And animals and really fussy babies.

One time, when I was struggling with feelings of guilt and unworthiness about growing a financially successful business, my coach, Makenna Held, said to me, "Your failure doesn't help dismantle White supremacy. But doing your work could."

I want to say a similar thing to you here. Your suffering and exhaustion don't help dismantle systems of oppression. These systems FEED on human suffering, yours included.

But you thriving? You full-on LIVING? Your heart over-flowing with love and your radiance shining out of your eyes and every pore of your being?

That is a force to be reckoned with.

Yes, we will need to do hard things sometimes.

And absolutely, if you hold a lot of privileges, especially White privilege, you'll need to let go of some comforts along the way. You'll need to be courageous. Without a doubt, your heart will still break at times. You'll feel discouraged and dismayed.

But also, you will find rest and peace. And you will feel beauty sink into your heart and nourish your soul. You will laugh and play and remember that living life is such a gift.

We'll talk more about how to increase your capacity to make an impact without falling into the traps of the grind culture in Part 2 of this book. But we're starting with you for a reason.

Want to ensure that the needs of the suffering are met? I'm suggesting here that you start by taking radical responsibility for making sure you're meeting your own. Want to change the world? Larissa Parson invites you to start as close to home as you can get. In your own body. We know that letting go of the push-harder-sacrifice-more mindset isn't easy. But neither is living in its grasp. If you like the idea of some new possibilities, keep reading.

JOY IS A REMEDY FOR INJUSTICE
WORKING WITH THE BODY AS A PLACE OF RESISTANCE

LARISSA PARSON

Author bio: Larissa Parson is a joy and justice coach, podcaster, and writer. She helps her clients move toward radical self-love, body liberation, and joy through group coaching, 1-1 support, and embodiment/movement classes. Larissa's intersectional identities include Black, biracial, queer, chronically ill, and mom to twins. She lives outside Durham, NC, on the traditional lands of the Eno, Tutelo, Saponi, Occaneechi, Shakori, and the Tuscarora people, in a country built on stolen bodies, lives, and labor.

Here's a radical idea: Your body is worthy of care and love, no matter what you do with it. And here's another: There is no justice without joy.

It's easy to be intellectual about justice, but injustice is acted upon the body; and joy, the bodily experience of pleasure, is a remedy for injustice. Leaning into joy is a way to work to change the world without focusing only on what's going wrong.

Like you, I really want to create change in the world. But as you may also have experienced, it's hard to work toward liberation when you're spending four hours every day hating on your own body.

The culture we live in systematically devalues us based on characteristics of our bodies. It has us thinking our bodies aren't worthy of love and safety, let alone joy! This message serves what actress and producer Laverne Cox (building on bell hooks) calls the cisnormative, heteronormative, imperialist, White supremacist, capitalist patriarchy by keeping us shopping, keeping women tired, keeping Black people sick and afraid, keeping law enforcement officers afraid and violent, and keeping everyone busy focusing on how their bodies need to change instead of living joyfully *in* their bodies.[1]

As a queer, bi-racial Black woman and mother living in the U.S., my journey with my body has been closely intertwined with my journey towards liberation — and joy. For years, I felt, as many women do, that if my body was just a little different, a little smaller, then I'd be worthy of love. Not just worthy of receiving love from someone else, but worthy of love from myself. It took making peace with chronic illness; a whole lot of reading, thinking and conversations; and even a career change(!) to stop listening to the voice that says, "You're not enough."

You are enough. I know it's hard to believe that, and that's where body liberation comes in.

Body liberation isn't something that happens overnight. It's a process of small steps. The more we take, the more free we get, and the more joy we start to experience.

How do we start? We start by noticing.

What do I mean by noticing? In this case, I mean to recognize which feelings and thoughts are yours and which ones belong to the system and can just fuck right off.

The goal of body liberation isn't to liberate yourself from having hard feelings about your body! No matter how much you practice, you might still have days when you don't love your body, when you're feeling angry with your body, when you're frustrated with your body. It's okay to have those feelings. My suggestion for you is that instead of judging the body, or the thoughts and emotions, you start to cultivate curiosity. Start noticing what your body desires, needs, and enjoys. Listen, then respond. Cultivating curiosity toward the body means that we don't run away from the difficult feelings, even while we embrace joy and pleasure.

To take an example from my own life, there have been times when I've felt compelled to show up and teach when my body was clearly saying, "NO." Rather than listen to my body's need for rest, I pushed through and showed up anyway, probably not at my best. That's internalized ableism at work, with just a hint of perfectionism/White supremacy culture.

Here's what I do now when the "just do it anyway" impulse shows up:

1. I get curious. Why does it feel important to show up? Who do I think I'm letting down by not showing up? What happens if I don't show up?
2. I look for the source. How much of showing up is a "should"? (i.e., it belongs to dominator culture, not me).
3. Then I ask: What does my body need?

4. After getting some clarity, I take action — cancel the thing, or plan for extra rest afterward, or do it anyway from a clear space of having chosen.

Choosing to cancel, to rest, to take care of my body first is a revolutionary act in a culture that prizes grinding our bodies to dust.

But when I come from a place of curiosity, I don't need to feel bad about my body's need to rest. And I'm able to sit with the waves of shame that wash over me without judgment, because I know they are not mine.

Being in your body isn't something you can avoid. The question is: HOW would you like to be in your body?

Me, I choose to enjoy the heck out of having my body. I choose to wake up every day secure that my body is worthy of love. And that means yours is, too. And so is every other body. When we start looking through the lens of love, we can change the world. And enjoy the process.

RESOURCES FOR YOUR JOURNEY

A COMMUNITY CONNECTION

The Slow Burn is an online community that will help you fall in love with yourself through movement, mindset, rest, and consciousness-raising cultivated by the one-and-only Larissa Parson.

PRACTICES TO TRY

1) Ready to stop making unreasonable demands? Try a time/joy diary.

Lots of people suggest tracking your time to see how you spend it. But when I started tracking my time, I didn't just want to know how I spent it, I wanted to know what tasks brought me joy and energized me, and which ones mostly just drained me. So, I added emotions to my time-tracking chart.

At the time I was a professor and here's what I found. Writing felt like joy/energy. Grading ALWAYS drained me. I could work a 50-hour week if most of it was writing, I felt joyful and energized most of the time. I could work 30 hours mostly grading and you would need to scrape me off the floor to get me to the dinner table.

When I first started working as a life coach, I found that I might feel drained going *into* a session, but I consistently felt energized *after* the session. Discovering what kind of work is an energy multiplier for me has radically changed my life.

Your time/joy diary doesn't need to be fancy. And it doesn't need to be perfect. Most often mine is barely legibly scratched onto a legal notepad. I don't manage to record my emotions with every activity. Here's an example:

7:30–9:00am Writing blog post — in flow

10:30am–2:00pm Website work — getting depressed

6:30–6:45pm Scrolling on Facebook — unsatisfying

9:00–10:00pm TV — eh

If you like more structure you can make an excel spreadsheet or download a time tracking app — as long as it has space for you to note how you feel and not just what you do. Make your own happy/sad face code. Whatever works.

The important thing is that you start to pay attention. Then start editing out the draining stuff as much as possible and add more energy-and-joy-multiplying activities into your days.

2) Want to move stress through and out of the body? Try shaking.

Shaking is a simple letting-go practice that can help you move stress through and out of the body. It's one of my favorites! You can shake systematically — one leg at time, then your hips, belly, shoulders, arms, and hands. You can also just *allow* your body to move and shake when it wants to, instead of stopping it, which we often do. And of course, turning on some music and shaking your booty can work too! As you do, imagine that you are inviting anything in your body that's ready to be released to fall to the earth where it can be composted to support future growth. [1]

AN ORGANIZATION TO FOLLOW

The Nap Ministry — founded by activist, artist, and theologian Tricia Hersey, the Nap Ministry promotes the view that rest is a form of resistance and reparations, and a challenge to the grind culture.

BOOKS

The Body Is Not An Apology and *Your Body Is Not An Apology Workbook* — Sonya Renee Taylor's invitation to "radical self-love" is a guide to making the world a place that is nourishing, safe, and respectful for all bodies, including yours.

The Artist's Way — This book had a huge impact on my life. It's a permission slip for the most vibrant (but likely starving) parts of you to start getting what you need. Definitely not just for artists.

2

YOU ARE ALREADY GOOD, AND YOU CAN'T GET IT ALL RIGHT — THAT'S NOT WHAT THIS WORK IS ABOUT (AND BESIDES, PERFECTIONISM IS A CHARACTERISTIC OF WHITE SUPREMACIST, PATRIARCHAL, CAPITALIST CULTURE)

AN INVITATION TO LIVE AS IF IT'S TRUE

I'm going to go out on a limb here and say it. You are already good. Not conditionally good. Like you did a good job. Not talented or skilled good. Like good at math. Good at soccer.

At. Your. Core. Good. And loved. Already deeply loved.

Pause and breathe in that possibility. Already good enough. Already loved.

What happens in your body? Do you cringe? Do you notice your jaw tightening? Do you feel tears welling up behind your eyes? Does your mind start creating a litany of reasons to show that you most definitely are NOT good?

If you're anything like me, at first you can't even imagine this possibility. Can't even pretend that you believe it.

Maybe you've internalized your "not goodness" from the messages of a culture that has told you from birth that the body that holds you, nourishes you, and gives you access to sex and taste, and the feel of water on your skin, and so many other pleasures, is somehow inherently wrong. Too dark. Too fat. Too disabled. Too female.

Maybe you hear your parent or a religious teacher saying, "Well, that's incredibly arrogant; no one is good but God."

Or perhaps you hear your mind say, "There's so much suffering in the world. I've even caused and benefitted from some of it. It's wrong for me to believe that I am good."

It can seem humble to believe in our "not goodness" to deflect praise. Particularly if you live as a woman, you will be commended for lifting others up and hiding your own radiance. You will be criticized if you demonstrate too much pride in your work or delight in your accomplishments, characteristics, and skills. But I want to put forth the possibility that your efforts to be good are not helping to create a more just, equitable, and inclusive world.

Why?

Because when we are trying to be good, we're in a constant state of judgment — needing to prove or defend our goodness. Often, we aren't fully conscious of this need, but it shows up in our harsh critiques of ourselves and others. It shows up in our defensive reactions when people point out that we've caused harm. It shows up in our exhausted bodies and weary hearts.

So much equity and justice work gets tangled up in some form of this question of goodness or rightness. I bet you know what I mean. It's pervasive in the "calling out" practices of cancel culture that cause us to look for who is more wrong than we are or cower in shame when we get called out or called in.

This "goodness" issue is a particular problem for White people doing social justice work because when we do not believe that, at our core, we are already good enough, we spend a whole lot of energy trying to prove that we are the "good White person." We require BIPOC people to agree with us that we are "good White people" — whether explicitly or implicitly. Or we get frozen in shame, overwhelm, or defensiveness, unable to take action.

The goodness issue comes up for BIPOC people as well, just in different forms. For one of my clients, it came up largely related to class. She grew up with far fewer resources than what she has now, and though she wanted to help young Black girls to find their way to a more abundant life, she kept getting stuck. When we dug a little deeper, part of what we hit was a belief that she really doesn't matter much. That shame had roots in negative experiences as a Black woman at a predominantly White institution in a male-dominated field. It made a lot of sense that not trying to do more — for herself or for young girls — seemed like a better option than trying and finding out she wasn't good enough.

Your unique intersecting identities and experiences will shape the form your "trying to be good" (or trying to avoid being bad or failing) takes, but I'm guessing some of this feels familiar to you too.

I'm not suggesting that we never DO bad things that we need to acknowledge and for which we need to make amends and/or ask for forgiveness. But I do wonder who and what benefits from so many of us living with these questions constantly running in the back of our minds: Am I being good? Are they being good? Are "my people" good? Are "my people" bad?

What if these are not the right questions to ask if we want to live with joy and delight? What if they don't help us to bring more equity and justice into the world either?

I'm not going to try to convince you that you're good-at-your-core good from a philosophical or religious, or humanist perspective. There are other places you can go for that. But I am going to invite you to consider the "what if?" of this possibility.

What if you are already good?

When I began to imagine this possibility for myself, here's what I found. I found that the love and healing I had to share with others expanded. I didn't become more arrogant as I feared. I became less easily activated and reactionary. I felt a deep sense of calm and an ability to accept other people as they are. They didn't have to think I was good, or loving, or right. They didn't have to be what I considered to be "right" for me to be able to hold a space of welcome for them. They were free to be fully themselves. I saw them relaxing into this acceptance and finding healing and rest, creating community, beauty, and laughter.

In the book *Just Mercy*, Bryan Stevenson says, "Each of us is more than the worst thing we've ever done" (17). If you're reading this, I'm guessing that you, like I, would love to see us abolish our harsh punitive surveillance systems of defining people by their worst choices and seeking to control people's actions through force from preschool until death. I imagine you'd like to see them replaced with systems rooted in community, regeneration, right relationships, reconciliation, and repair.

Well, Amazing One, I have a hunch that abolition starts right in your very own body, mind, and heart — as you shift your internal system from one of punishment and exile of the parts you don't like, to one of deep love and acceptance for all of you, without exception.

Want to let go of the good/bad binary? You'll undoubtedly be encouraged by the story Trevia Woods shares about how she's walking the path of developing a positive racial identity that engages with the uncomfortable histories that shape her story (and ours).

HOW CAN WE HAVE A POSITIVE RACIAL IDENTITY NO MATTER WHO OUR ANCESTORS WERE?

TREVIA WOODS

Author bio: Trevia (TREE-va) Woods is a mixed-race woman with Indigenous ancestors and nearly two decades of experience in body-work, education, and community-building. She has roots in the Midwest and Colorado and has traveled the world. Trevia hosts the HELD community helping people remember their power by learning to establish traditions and community care rituals while connecting with their own lineage and heritages without culturally or spiritually appropriating.

How can we have a positive racial identity no matter who our ancestors were? This question is something that I have been working through and reframing in my body for many years. The key is expanding our ability to hold multiple, complex, and uncomfortable truths in our bodies.

When we think about the multiple identities of race, sexual orientation, gender, body type, and class, we can see how our own identities are complex. For example, I am queer, fat, mixed-race, woman, and middle class (presently). All of these identities inform my perspective of the world, and also influence how others might accept and treat me.

I hold two very heavy truths in my body.

On the one hand, my maternal line has some ancestors that were Indigenous to Turtle Island. This line has seen the very acute effects of colonization. The intergenerational trauma and displacement from our community has been devastating. Figuring out how to navigate being a mixed-race person without ties to my Indigenous community has been fraught with a sense of never being enough in almost every group I have interacted with.

On the other hand, by studying my family tree, I learned that it's likely that some of my ancestors are from North Carolina and a few owned enslaved people. Literally, some of my ancestors stole the life, bodies, and labor of other people to get a leg up from their own circumstances. Having felt some discrimination for being a mixed-race person and having my own traditions and communities stripped from my family, this knowledge cuts deeply. It's very uncomfortable.

Expanding my capacity for holding those uncomfortable feelings in my body has led me to a greater sense of belonging and acceptance of myself and my lineage. Taking a moment to pause and allow these truths to be noticed and acknowledged instead of hiding or trying to release them; breathing through the urge to push them down or away. This embodied way of integrating my identities is the work that has been most transformative for me. One resource I used was *My Grandmother's Hands* by Resmaa Menakem. I learned a lot from both reading and DOING the activities in this book. It was one among many texts and practices that helped me learn to get comfortable with breathing through the pause and letting go of the binary.

When we let go of the binary of good vs. bad, our ancestors become human beings with traits we can admire while also acknowledging the harm they caused. They can be rich in identities just like we are. For example, my grandma was a fat, Indigenous, female, blue collar, abuse survivor who frankly made a fool of herself when she drank. She did change course as she got older and rarely drank, but my point is that she was wise and flawed and I loved her beyond measure.

Where our lineage includes people who caused harm, or were part of the group that was in power and oppressed others, we can be honest about the privilege we gained. And we can acknowledge that they were living their lives within a flawed system that pits humans against humans. Where our lineage includes people who were oppressed and harmed, we can grieve our losses, learn their stories and tell them with pride.

We can also begin to understand that our ancestors and current living relations have wisdom for us to learn from and lessons for us to heed.

In my own life (and body) I've found that when I can find peace and truth within my lineage, I can find it also within myself. I invite you on the same journey. The only way forward is truth and facing the uncomfortable feelings it brings up. From there we can move forward to a world filled with more justice and belonging. Our best classroom is each other; let's do this, together.

RESOURCES FOR YOUR JOURNEY

A COMMUNITY CONNECTION

Get inspired to find your Radical Self-Truth by signing up for Trevia Woods' monthly newsletter Unfurl. Even better, join the next cohort of HELD — learn more on her website www. manytreeslifeway.com.

PRACTICES TO TRY

1) Embrace the path of celebration and acknowledgement as an act of resistance — or just to make your life easier!

One of the simplest and most important practices you can add into your daily life (and share with kids!) is celebration. Not big celebrations like birthdays and graduations, though those are delightful, but regular little celebrations of imperfect and seemingly unimportant accomplishments.

I first learned about this practice from Katherine North but pretty much every coach I know uses it — including me. Dr.

B. J. Fogg, who runs the Behavior Design Lab at Stanford, found that when seeking to change habits, celebrating makes success in the future more likely because your body and brain feel all celebrations as being equally significant. Big or small, celebrating feels good. Working hard and never feeling like we're finished (or good enough) doesn't. So, one reason to celebrate is because it makes hard changes easier. And because perfectionism is a known characteristic of White supremacist culture, celebration is also a powerful act of resistance. So next time you take a small step, celebrate yourself! Do something physical like a fist pump or jumping up and down that will let your brain and body know it's worth it to do all that hard work! Even better, share your successes with someone else.

2) Create your own personal self-compassion mantra.

The next time you screw up somehow, or just wish you were stronger, smarter, saner, more organized, had a better body, or whatever it is on that particular day, say to yourself what the best, kindest version of you would say to a child in your situation. Write it on a card, or make a note in your phone. Repeat as needed.

3) Try a DIY version of the practice I did above.

Imagine a recent situation in which you felt defensive because it seemed as if someone was saying (or implying) that you aren't good/good enough. Now imagine that a golden light begins to shine down from above you — into your mind, then your heart, slowly warming you all the way down to your toes. Feel the warmth of it around the base of your spine and in your lower belly. Feel that this warm light has a message. "You are already good. You are already good enough." When you can really feel that possibility, look back at the situation you started with. Notice what, if anything changes. If your mind has lots of objections, great! Now you know where you have some limiting beliefs you can question. If you felt the possibility of this golden light truth, even just for a fleeting moment, if you saw how it might change situations in your life, also great! In either case, keep coming back to the practice as a meditation.

4) Take intentional steps toward forming a racial and cultural identity that acknowledges the whole of who you are, complicated as that may be.

Learn about your lineage. Acknowledge your ancestors' pain and their mistakes. Get support when it gets hard, which happens whether you're learning about people who caused harm, or those who were harmed. Look for the joy and resilience in their stories. Let go of labeling them good/bad or distancing yourself. You're connected. Embrace the mess of being human.

BOOKS

My Grandmother's Hands by Resmaa Menakem is a manual for compassion and courage. It explains how racial trauma gets stuck in our bodies — looking specifically at White bodies, Black bodies and Police bodies — and provides practices to help you process that trauma instead of being controlled by it.

As Trevia mentioned, it's not a book to read, but one to practice, preferably in community.

The Gifts of Imperfection by Brene Brown. This is one of her earlier books, but it's still my favorite. If you struggle with shame and perfectionism, it's a great place to start.

3

THE PATH TOWARDS FEELING BETTER IS LEARNABLE — YOU HAVE THE POWER TO CHOOSE IT

Here's the good news. And the bad news. Your ability to feel better in and about your life isn't dependent on anyone else. It's up to you to take responsibility for it. If you're feeling weighed down by life, it's not your partner's fault, your kids' fault, or your mother's fault. It's not your fault either — this isn't about blame — but you are the one who can change your experience.

Wait! Don't stop reading! I know this can sound like really bad news, like a task that's impossible and unfair. I get it. In the first coaching program I was in, about halfway through, there was a week during which we were supposed to cultivate JOY! My reaction was to feel enraged. "WTF! That's the one thing I CAN'T do! So unfair!" I knew I could attack problems, like my unorganized finances or my cluttered closet, but to experience joy? To play? Not possible.

I know you don't need one more impossible task on your never-ending "to-do" list, so why do I say this is good news? Here's why. Because (as you may have noticed) no matter how hard you try, you can't control other people. Nor can you fix the past or predict the future. So, if your happiness depends on any of these, you're likely to live with a lot of fear and frustration. Just accepting that you can't control much of life can be a big stress reliever in itself. Though I know, it's not that easy to do.

What I want you to know is that you can control a lot of what will make you feel better. There are skills you can learn and steps you can take that will help you to experience life more consistently from a place of joy, delight, gratitude, love — and any other number of "feel good" emotions. There are even ways you can increase your capacity to ride the waves of more challenging emotions like anger, grief, and discouragement so they don't stay stuck in your body and your heart. (We'll touch on them a bit in the next chapter.)

Curious? Doubtful? Ready to give me the benefit of the doubt? Well then, I invite you to do a little experiment with me right now.

Think about some time in the recent past (preferably today) when you said or thought something that started with one of the following phrases.

"I can't..."

"I don't have time to..."

"I should..."

"I have to..."

Now, say the thought out loud to yourself and notice how you feel in your body — see if you can place it. Is it a tightness in your stomach? A burning sensation in your heart? A heaviness on your shoulders? If you can't feel anything in your body, notice the tone of your voice. Do you sound empowered? Strong? Whiney? Resentful? Tired?

Then replace the original statement with one that includes some version of the word "choose."

"I choose not to…"

"I chose not to…"

"I choose to…"

"I am choosing…"

Notice how it feels in your body to make this new statement. Often people say they feel an expansion in their chest, a lightness as if a weight has been lifted, or a feeling of being grounded and centered in their lower belly. Usually, the tone of their voice deepens and strengthens. Why do these small word changes lead to such bit shifts? Because… changing your language in this way shifts the power source for your life away from circumstances you can't control back to you. And having more power over your life *feels better.*[1]

It's true. You don't have all the choices you may want in life. But you always have choices. And sure, sometimes it may be uncomfortable to take ownership of the choice you're making, but it will also feel true. In my experience, truth feels good in the body.

Creating a few new patterns of speech in your everyday language is one of the fastest, simplest, and most effective steps you can take towards feeling less overwhelmed by life. You may be surprised at how quickly you notice a shift in your energy levels, your outlook, and your ability to see new possibilities.

Of course, choosing to find ways to add in more of what you love and letting go of activities that are energy drains for you, as we talked about in Chapter 1, is also supportive of feeling better. (Did you try the time/joy diary yet?) Even if those changes are tiny, you'll be amazed at how those tiny steps — 10 minutes of dancing here, saying "no" to a request there — add up to a life that feels more like one that was made for you. At the end of this chapter, there are a couple more ideas and resources you can check out that will help you (slowly, slowly, gently, gently) to strengthen your "feel better" muscles.

But first, I have to warn you that as you get moving down this path, you are very likely to encounter some resistance. Voices in your head that tell you you're being selfish, or you really can't, or some other version of, "Don't bother trying." Don't worry, Marquita Davis is here to help you navigate those murky waters and find your way to the other side.

EXCUSE ME MA'AM, BUT YOU DROPPED SOME CRITICISM IN MY DAY!

MARQUITA DAVIS

Author bio: Marquita Davis is a freelance writer based in Philadelphia, Pennsylvania, who believes that fluency with our own emotions strengthens our ability to connect with others. Her work highlights the importance of understanding ourselves, our traumas, and triggers as a path to healing and authentic living. She plans to build on this work, with a little humor, when possible as she explores the field of life coaching.

Have you ever had a good feeling about something you did or planned when suddenly there was an internal murmur speaking against it, trying to tell you *all* the reasons why you shouldn't? The self-development world refers to that voice as an "inner critic." I'm going to try and unpack a little bit of what that means.

Inner critics show up in different forms. One way mine shows up is as a character I call "The Mean Lunch Lady." She shows up complete with a bonnet, hair curlers, lipstick applied all too thickly on pursed lips struggling to keep control of a cigarette with an inch of ashes poised to fall onto my lunch tray as she serves criticism of nearly everything while slamming my tray with lumpy, cold mashed potatoes. I don't know about you, but yikes!

You probably experience your inner critic differently, but we all have one. Our inner critics are the voices inside us that lead us to weighty internal struggles when we try to move forward, to act on inspired ideas, or to develop consistency and momentum towards the lives we want.

I know this doesn't sound like a pleasant person to have hanging around in your head, but it's not one we need to fear or try to evict. It may be hard to believe, but the critic is the part of you that is most concerned with your safety. The problem is it screams just as loud whether the danger it senses is physical or emotional, real or imagined.

At the time of this writing, I've not discerned any method that's made my critic mute or 100 percent satisfied. But I have gained some understanding that I will share hoping they encourage you to have the final say over your inner critic through action.

1. The inner critic is part of you, but it's not you.
It's a thin line, but it's there — that line that separates us from our inner critics. The voice is so familiar it can feel like it's all of who we are, but you can learn to recognize yours. Our critics often speak in absolutes and wild "what if" scenarios. True story, my critic once had me convinced my children would perish of neglect if I decided to attend a weekly poetry event. Time away from home, including travel, two hours, max. Even though they were of age to feed themselves (young teens), even though there was another adult (their father) in

the home while I was gone, the critic criticized. She told me I was being selfish doing something for myself that would take away from my responsibility to my family and home. She hit me where I lived with that one.

2. The critic is a master of camouflage.
Now, on the surface, the critic's concern seems genuine. Afterall, who wouldn't be concerned for the welfare of their loved ones. However, the critic and I have the same set of facts and understandings as it relates to the capabilities of my folks at home to fend for themselves while I was away. The critic never said "boo" when I was away for overtime or a part-time job, but she had an objection when I wanted to do something for myself, something new, something that was a departure from the "norm" of how other people knew me. Those can all be a bit scary, which is why my favorite curmudgeon disguised her attempt to keep me safe in my box by preying on my fear of being a bad mom. Crafty, ain't she?

3. The Critic is not your enemy.
Fighting with it won't get you closer to your goals. When the inner critic part of you raises awareness of phantom traumas, it's only trying to preserve your current existence because your current existence feels safe — which leads me to my next point...

4. The Critic needs to be heard and accepted.
Your Inner Critic doesn't speak for nothing. It may sound silly, but simply asking my critic to name the fear at the root of her complaint has often helped me to find new ways forward. Understand your critic is afraid, find out why, and offer comfort by speaking directly to the heart of the critic's concern. In this instance, my critic feared my embarrassment

and rejection because I'd never shared much of my writing up to that point.

5. The Critic is not all-knowing.
The voice that recites past failures and potential calamities as proof of why you absolutely must not do X, *"Because of what happened to that one person that one time they tried something different, and it led to the ruin of all..."* (to be read in one breath really fast), is not anybody's expert in anything!

6. You get to decide when to listen.
The report and testimony of the critic in our heads only holds the sway we allow. We no more need to follow the misguidance of our inner critic than we do that of an external person dictating our actions. Assigning your critic its own identity, imagining it as a character like I did, is a great way to set your critic apart as one you can engage with, and not just be chastised by.

You'll remember me saying earlier that I've not effectively muted my critic. You might be surprised to know that she's right here with me typing these words. I know this may sound indulgent as coping mechanisms go, but if you'll allow me a few more sentences, I'd like to share some parting words from her with you.

POST SCRIPT FROM MARQUITA'S CRITIC, AKA THE MEAN LUNCH LADY

Hey, you! Yes, you! I learned she's writing this because you're thinking about doing something new or different. Well, I've come to warn ya (cue scoop of potatoes) STAY THE SAME... (plop) NEVER CHANGE! Cuz if ya do, you'll be different! ... And if you're different, then the world would be different. And you want everything to stay the same, don't ya? Yes, the world is just fine the way it is... Don't ever be or do different! (plop.) Lunch Lady, Out!

RESOURCES FOR YOUR JOURNEY

A COMMUNITY CONNECTION

Head over to innermestories.com and sign up to receive weekly stories from Marquita Davis where she shares writings meant to encourage and shares joys she's discovered with meditation (and I'm pretty sure she'll have you laughing out loud too!).

PRACTICES TO TRY

1) Edit your everyday vocabulary, make room for your power.

Don't take my word for it, continue doing the experiment above and see how it feels to own your choices. You can always go back to "I can't" and "I don't have time" if you like it better.

2) Every day for a week, do a small, not-very-time-or-money-consuming activity that feels ridiculous, but gives you a slight pang of joy — like a kid might get rolling down a grassy hill just for the pleasure of it, not because it makes any sense.

Show that inner part of yourself that is currently on the verge of starving that you actually care — that they finally get to eat now (even while there are still lots of things on your 'to do' list). Here are a couple possibilities:

- Buy yourself flowers, or the expensive chocolate bar, or fancy organic whatever-it-is that excites you — and don't pick up anything for anyone else at the same time.
- Read that trashy magazine.
- Dance in the kitchen.
- Climb a tree or swing on a swing.
- Eat dessert first.
- Play with Play-Doh.
- Get in your car and make silly faces at yourself in the mirror.
- Actually hug a tree.

Notice the impact on your body and emotions. My hunch is that something will shift for you — just a little bit. Bonus if you share your experience with a friend.

3) Create a character for your inner critic, like Marquita did.

It helps if it's humorous. Make sure even if the voice sounds like your grumpy mother-in-law or your third grade teacher, or yourself, you create a character a little less close to an actual human. Some people in the coach world call the inner critic your lizard brain, given its connection to the part of your brain that is focused on survival. If it's easier for you than creating a character from your own imagination, you might google lizard pictures and see if you can find one that fits. The next time you hear that voice in your head, get a little distance from it by naming it. "Oh, my inner lizard/lunch lady/Oscar the Grouch is talking." If the voice is really loud, and you're getting stuck, you might imagine giving it a snack, or sending it on a little vacation, while you continue to take action in the direction of your dreams.

A BOOK

Tara Mohr's *Playing Big* is one of my favorites for women who want DIY life coaching that will help you to dismantle internalized sexism and find your power to choose the life you want. The first chapter focuses on the Inner Critic.

4

TO LEARN HOW TO FOLLOW THE PATH TOWARDS FEELING BETTER, YOU'RE GOING TO NEED TIME, AND SOME NEW GUIDES

Since you're here, my guess is, in some way, you're "surviving" life. That's a good thing. I, for one, am glad that you are alive! You've probably even had some big wins — kids you're proud of, a degree you worked hard for, a letter from a student who would have dropped out if it hadn't been for you — or maybe you led the charge to bring about a change in your community that's having a significant ongoing impact. Whatever your wins, I'm right here celebrating them with you.

Here's the problem. Now that you want to shift from surviving to thriving, the very useful practices, beliefs, and habits that were your guides up to this point — characters like Perfectionism, Push Harder, Stay Small, and Stiff Upper Lip — don't know the way to Feel Better. You're charting new territory.

I have two invitations for you in this chapter. The first is to give yourself some time and space as you experience the discomfort that comes with trying new ways of operating in the world. The second is to start following some new guides.

The three I'll introduce here aren't the only options, but they will get you started.

INVITATION #1: GIVE YOURSELF THE TIME AND SPACE YOU NEED TO MAKE THE CHANGES YOU WANT.

Sometimes change is easy. Enjoy it if that's your experience! But, if you've been trying some of the suggested practices from the first three chapters and you're not exactly on top of the world, you're not doing it wrong. In times of significant transition, there's much letting go that needs to happen — of past trauma, outdated beliefs, or relationships that are no longer supportive. As that purging and releasing is happening, it can be uncomfortable.

There may be bodily discomfort. You might literally (or energetically, as I have done a couple of times now) throw up. Your body might want to shake involuntarily to complete a stress cycle from a past trauma that you never fully processed or develop a strange rash to let go of something it's been holding onto. This is all totally within the realm of normal. The body is amazing at letting go of stuff when we allow it. Of course, you should keep in touch with health professionals who can help your body to heal, but I want you to know that these are pretty common reactions.

There will undoubtedly be emotional discomfort, too. Perhaps you'll feel angry or sad but can't quite explain it based on your current circumstances. There may be waves of grief as you let go of painful events from your past, unmet expectations, or even beautiful chapters of your life that have ended. There will likely be fear as you make choices that don't align with what other people think you "should" do. You may even notice (as I did) that you feel uncomfortable relaxing or feeling playful, so allowing yourself to feel good could be uncomfortable at first. Ride the waves. Emotions are meant to flow.

Your relationships will change too. Some will reshape to make room for the expanded version of you. Some won't go with you into the next phase. Life coach Martha Beck calls this experience "the empty elevator syndrome" — as in, you're going to a new level, and the people who were with you at the start keep getting out on the floors below. For a while, it's just you in there alone, and you wonder if you'll be alone forever. Don't worry; you won't.

I share all of this to say, feeling worse in some ways is often part of the journey towards feeling better, like the sore muscles you get when you try a new workout. My suggestion is that you see the discomfort as an invitation to be gentle with yourself and give it time. Urgency is also part of the oppressive cultural context we live in; slowing down and trusting the process is the remedy.

Now, to introduce you to three of my favorite guides on the road to thriving...

INVITATION #2: FOLLOW NEW GUIDES.

Recommended Guide #1 — Your body

Yup. That "meat sack" that carries around your brain? It has its own wisdom. If you've been discounting the wisdom of your body, you probably can't hear most of what it's trying to tell you. Or you hear it and ignore it. That sick feeling in your stomach when you said "yes" to that event you don't want to attend — it has something to tell you! Maybe it's, "Don't go," or maybe it's, "This is going to be BIG for you, get ready!" or something else. The first step to harvesting this vast wisdom is to notice that it's available.

Recommended Guide #2 — Your emotions — especially the uncomfortable ones

Since the Age of Enlightenment, Reason has ruled as king of all decision-making in many cultures. So, it's likely you've been impacted by the bias against emotions as sources of wisdom. This bias is gendered and racialized. Feeling emotions has been a strength of feminine energy (often stronger in women), and emotional expression was much more common in many of the cultures that were deemed to be "uncivilized" during the age of colonization. Views denigrating emotional expression helped to justify colonization and exclude women from positions of power. So, let's turn that ship around, shall we?

First, keep noticing your joy and corresponding desires, as you started to do in Chapter One. There's so much goodness available when you follow joy and desire.

Next, start choosing to feel the more uncomfortable emotions that you tend to avoid — like jealousy, resentment, anger, and grief. A note of caution: Before you go crazy vomiting your anger on your loved ones and blaming it on me, let me remind you that feeling your emotions doesn't require that you allow them to take over! You can learn how to feel them, let your body express them, listen to the message they have for you, and then choose what action you want to take. You are still in charge; you're just adding them to your table of advisors.

Recommended Guide #3 — Your Inner Wisdom

One reason I love being alive at this time in history is that science is now starting to catch up to what many of us have experienced — the logical linguistic left side of our brain doesn't know everything. In fact, it misses out on huge amounts of information that get collected by the right side of the brain, by our gut (sometimes called our "second brain"), and other parts of our body. There's even information that's encoded in our DNA from the experiences of our ancestors.[1] Intuitive knowing doesn't come out of nowhere.

Different people feel and find their inner truth in different ways. For a very small number of people, intuition might not be a strength, but for a lot of us, it is. And it's a hugely under-utilized resource. The best way I know to strengthen your trust in yours is to experiment with following it and then reflect on the outcome. Sometimes you'll make mistakes, but truth be told, have you always been happy with the choices you made based on a logical analysis of the pros and cons?

You can also seek outside supports to help you to connect with your inner wisdom. Working with skilled coaches has been a key part of my journey, as have meditation and prayer. Some less mainstream practices I've found helpful include oracle deck readings, consultations with healers who can connect with spirit guides, and plant journeys with trusted trained facilitators, but you don't have to go that route if you don't want to.

And please know that I'm not telling you to stop thinking! I LOVE my mind! Without it, this book would not exist. But as many of my teachers have told me, and as I have seen for myself and my clients, the mind is more effective as a supporter than as a leader. It helps me analyze, synthesize, and figure out steps forward *once I know where I'm heading*. But if it thinks it's in charge, I tend to end up running in circles of confusion and fear.

Not sure this touchy-feely, non-rational approach is for you? My husband (and the only male contributor to this book!) David Valentine wasn't exactly a prime candidate for all this heart-body stuff. His emotions were so far under wraps that our sons and I often used to have trouble distinguishing between his "really excited" expression and "I don't really care." But his love for all of us and an innate desire to find more meaning in life (as evidenced by an obsession with The *Lord of the Rings* and other transformation stories) led him to follow unexpected paths and find unexpected benefits. We hope his journey will inspire you on yours.

TRUE FREEDOM COMES FROM LEARNING TO ENJOY THE JOURNEY

DAVID V. VALENTINE

Author bio: David V. Valentine has spent most of his career in the world of private philanthropy and higher education finance and administration, where he consistently diversifies the workforce and mentors leaders (some out of the organization!). On the side, he loves to support transformative education and is currently exploring possibilities in the realm of spiritual direction and coaching.

It may sound cliché, but on my path to being my full self, I've realized that life is more about the journey than the destination. I've lived most of my life as a task oriented, left-brain kind of person. While I have been successful in that space, it has been my zone of excellence, not of genius. Lately, I feel like my creative and emotional sides are pushing at the seams to come out. More freedom and abundance are emerging as I follow new paths.

One of the first journeys I started on, over 20 years ago, was to go to counseling. I've found deep value in this practice which is not usually embraced by or offered to Black men.

Finding a Black male therapist isn't easy to do. I have never worked with one. It's worth it, though, when you find the right person. Initially, I went to therapy and participated at varied levels of engagement. Then there was the time we went to family counseling for almost a year when our oldest son was struggling, and the therapist ONLY TALKED WITH ME for most of each session! He invited me into deeper levels of engagement and connection, which helped me become a much better father to my sons. Currently my therapy sessions are focused on accessing and feeling my emotions and gaining skills to talk about what I am feeling, instead of what I am thinking.

Another one of my journeys was to deepen my connection with my extended families, both adoptive and birth. I got a greater sense of family history and connection to my southern roots. I had a privileged life and didn't feel a need to find my birth parents until I was around 50, when I started to engage in the process of understanding who I was as a Black man in America. I had my original birth certificate and knew my birth mother was from Virginia. This led to a Google search and eventually to me meeting her. That was the start of a year of family reunions — in Virginia, Arkansas, California, and Georgia, with family members from my birth and adoptive families. There's lots more to tell, but one of the most important things for me is that I now feel connected to the history, the people, and the land where my ancestors lived. Expanding my family connections has given me a much broader sense of self and a deeper story to tell about who I am and where I've come from.

Finally, my journey of discovery of who I was made to be has taken me away from some familiar aspects of my life and invited me to return to others. Having lived in Philadelphia all my life, at age 48, I moved to California. I don't think I could have grown in the ways I have without moving. It gave me the freedom to expand my sense of who I could be and what was possible. Even though I've now returned to the East Coast, I didn't return to Philly, though I'm not too far away. When I was in California, I experienced another important return. I found myself spending most of my days at a Black-owned creative workspace, founded by fellow Alphas. After years of living and working in predominantly White spaces, the time I spent there, just being Black and comfortable in my skin, was of incalculable benefit.

My journey has included lots of uncomfortable emotions, and I agree with Deb that you should expect them to come. But know that there won't only be discomfort; there will also be a whole lot of joy along the way. And if you're a man reading this, don't be afraid to pursue working with things that society tells us are feminine. You will experience a fuller life — as a whole (masculine/feminine) integrated person.

RESOURCES FOR YOUR JOURNEY

A Community Connection

Reach out to David at davidv06@gmail.com if you are a guy who is uncomfortable finding his way to his emotions. There's wholeness waiting for you.

Practices to Try

1) Walk from here to there — SLOWLY — even just a couple times a day.

Do it with the intention of honoring all that your body is doing. Do it as a way to say "no" to urgent, pushing energy. Do it as an embodied prayer, if that resonates for you. Notice what happens in your body and emotions when you do.

2) As noted above, Step 1 in hearing your body's wisdom is to believe that it has some. Step 2 is to notice what your body typically does when it likes something and what it does when it doesn't.

Most often people experience the body's "no" as contraction, tightness, pain, or heaviness and a "yes" is often a feeling of expansion, lightness, opening up, relaxing, or release. Step 3 is to get curious. Ask that sick feeling in your stomach, "Why are you here?" Ask the tightness in your jaw, "What do you need from me?" Your body may answer with a memory, a sensation, an emotion, or with words. Or maybe you won't hear an answer at all — remember this is a PRACTICE. Step 4 if you do hear an answer, see what you can do to meet the need, or respond to the insight you just got.[1]

3) Make it a habit to care for your body all the time.

Give it a little massage, drink water, take a bath, move it around, slow down to notice the food you eat, imagine the nourishment entering all your cells. Go to the bathroom when you need to go to the bathroom. Your body is amazing and it deserves to be cared for!

4) Feel your feelings.

Resentment is a particularly fabulous teacher for those of us who lack firm boundaries and tend to overgive (see Chapter 6 for more). Here's a practice to help you follow its guidance (but it can be adapted for other emotions).

Step 1: When you notice resentment rising, pause. Assume that it's a gift, a warning sign coming to alert you that you are off track.

Step 2: Just feel it. This step is so simple, but SO hard to do in the moment. Notice where you feel the resentment in your body and what it feels like. Name the sensations if you can. Most emotions last about 90 seconds. They are like ocean waves. They intensify and then they die back down — if we allow ourselves to stay in our BODIES and feel them. Examples of sensations are heat, contraction, vibrating — do an internet search for more sensations if you need help.[2]

Step 3: If possible, let your body move or sound the way that it wants to based on this sensation. Depending on where you are, options could be stomping, shaking your fists, screaming (even if you have to whisper yell into your pillow; cars are great for this too). Keep going until you come to a point where you feel the energy start to calm.

Step 4: Take a deep breath and look back. Notice when you gave what you did not want to give, or maybe what you wanted to give, but just didn't have the ability to give in that moment.

Step 5: Reflect or journal for a bit looking for the "should" that's usually lurking behind the choice you made — the place where you decided you "had" to do whatever it was. Once you find it, get curious about this "truth." Ask yourself:

- Where did this "should" come from?
- Did I think I had no choice? (Because we always have a choice. We may not like the alternatives, but we always have a choice.)
- What might I do differently if I thought I had other options?
- What other options might there be that are within my control?

Step 6: Take responsibility for the choice you made. Let go of blaming other people.

Step 7: Shift course based on what you learn. Take action if one is needed.

An Invitation to Invest in Support

In my experience, learning to follow the wisdom of your body, emotions, and intuition usually requires some extra support and quite a bit of practice. It's a core aspect of my work with clients. If this is an area of challenge for you, I'd love to connect to see if what I offer might be just what you need. You can find me at www.thriving4equity.com.

PART 2

DO BETTER

DO BETTER

Note: I don't actually love the phrase "do better" because it brings to mind an image of someone shaking a finger in my face. Still, you're here because you have some ideas about ways you want to make the world better for others. And the phrase lines up nicely with "feel better." But please know that there is no finger-pointing happening over here!

In many ways, the division between the two sections of this book is a bit arbitrary. In fact, you may have noticed that as you start feeling better, you become a person who loves bigger, who manages unexpected events with more ease, and who solves problems with more creativity. These are all examples of what I mean when I say that feeling better helps you to do better.

Also, taking steps to increase your capacity to make change in the world will also help you feel better. In reality, your "feeling better" and "doing better" are interwoven aspects of living fully from a place of integrity.

Integrity often gets talked about as a moral or ethical state, but primarily it is a reference to being in a state of completeness, being whole. I also see it as a place of being in alignment with what is true. And part of what is true for us right now on Planet Earth is that there are powerful systems of oppression and disrespect causing incredible harm.

If you're a person who feels that you really aren't doing much or enough, and you feel waves of shame as you read this, this section is for you. It will help you start to increase your capacity to take action in the ways you're called to, to let go of beating yourself up for not doing things that really aren't yours, and to distinguish between the two.

If you're a person who is powering through and making a big difference already but are concerned that you might be on the road to burning out or selling out, this section (along with the first one) is preventative medicine.

I believe it's time for us to start living from new paradigms. I believe we can dismantle old structures and systems based on shame and guilt, criticism and judgment, and fear and lack. I believe we can create new ones built on foundations of acceptance, love, and abundance. But I don't think we do it just from our meditation cushions or spiritual retreats. Neither do you. So let's start exercising some muscles you might not even know you had. And let's gently invite some tight ones to relax, so you can stretch into new places of courage and kindness.

5

BUT HOW WILL WE GET ANYTHING
DONE? PLEASURE AS A PARTNER TO
PRODUCTIVITY

In preparation for writing this chapter, I put my money where my mouth was and dove into pleasure. That is, in order to produce something, I played.

Backward right? Aren't we supposed to work first, then play? Do your homework, stay quiet and behave, and *then* you can go to recess? God forbid that you should move your body when it wants to move. Or eat when you are hungry, or sleep when you are tired. Produce art just because you want to? Lie down and feel the warmth of the sun? Enough of that. We have work to do.

In capitalist systems, humans are expected to produce — whether that's physical products, children, or profits. When you look closely at American public schools, it's not hard to see that they were built to shape children into good factory workers. Bells, schedules, the focus on compliance — all perfect conditioning for life on an assembly line.

Well, I don't love the capitalist system, but I also don't think it's going anywhere in my lifetime. And I think we can challenge it in multiple creative ways because we are infinitely creative beings, we humans.

One of those ways, the one I'm sharing here, is by prioritizing pleasure in the process of creation over pushing to produce. I can share from my own experience and that of my clients that shifting priorities in this way tends to improve production as well. Why? Because increasing pleasure in your life increases your power. Pleasure creates energy in your body that you can use, which increases your capacity to meet the goals you set for yourself — if that's how you want to use all the extra juiciness your pleasure creates for you.

And it's not just for this chapter that I've been trying out this new path towards productivity. I've been committed to a whole-life experiment with pleasure for a while now. And when I say pleasure, I also mean its companions — delight, love, trust, gratitude, fun, play, and magic, to name a few. I'm writing this book with fun, pleasure, excitement, love, and freedom infused into the whole process. I hope you can feel it!

This is a very different path than the one I followed to complete my dissertation several years ago. That path, which was peppered with all-nighters and way more yelling at my kids than I like to admit, was one in which I ignored my body's needs so much that I started having recurring dreams about nutritious soup and ended up writing the last few chapters uncomfortably in a recliner chair with ice on my back because I could barely move.

I know how to focus and push harder to produce. I bet you do too. And those are valuable skills. Don't get me wrong. The high that comes from working hard and getting what you were working for is fabulous too. It's just that we've gotten way out of balance in making use of these energies, often associated with masculine energy (which can be awesome but becomes toxic when it reigns unchecked as it has done for the past several centuries), without weaving in complementary (more feminine) energies of flow, pleasure, and surrender to the process.

Here's what this new way of working looked like for me today.

First, I walked to the local coffee shop and bought a latte and a Meyer lemon bergamot pastry that was divine. This may sound like no big deal if a latte is a daily affair for you, but for me, it's extra pleasure-filled because I don't indulge all that often. That's a tip for you: Sometimes having *less* of something brings *more* pleasure.

I was already excited about this day because I had no other commitments, and I knew I could dive deep into the writing process without distractions. The chance to go all-in rather than dancing between tasks is a delight for me, too. I lit some candles to acknowledge the start of what I consider to be a whole day of sacred work (another pleasure), put an away message on my email (fun!), and moved my phone to another room (avoiding distractions can increase both pleasure AND focus!).

After my latte and lemon delight, I took it up a notch and moved into some self-pleasuring with the intention of firing up my heart and fueling this writing process with more plea-sure. I started with meditative breathwork focused on self-love, then transitioned to a practice called "sex magic."[1] Stay with me here — we're not going X-rated! In this process, you take any kind of pleasurable sensation — for me today, it was mostly the pleasure of stretching and massaging tight muscles in my neck and jaw — and cycle it through each chakra, eventually sending it out of the top of your head with an image of what you desire. It's like prayer on pleasure steroids. You let the prayer-desire connect with the Universe/God and rain back down on you. Some people really feel the energy moving when doing this practice. I don't yet, but I still find it enjoyable.

Next up, I paused to comfort some parts of me that started freaking out because, "We are wasting this whole day, and we need to get to work!" I acknowledged the concern, put my hands on my tight jaw for a while, and breathed slowly through my nose. Providing honor, respect, and comfort to parts of me that are uncomfortable — whether those parts are physical, emotional, spiritual, or mental — is also pleasure.

Grateful for the attention, my worried parts calmed enough for me to move on to a bit of "regular" self-pleasuring (aka masturbation), after which I considered a nap but went for music and a bit more meditation. A piece of music came on that conjured images in my head of a bird soaring through the air (like Angelina Jolie as Maleficent when she got her wings back), so I got up and stretched my arms up and down as if I were the bird. Which also felt amazing. My body REALLY likes stretching these days.

After that, it was back to the pleasures of food. I cut up half an orange and admired the beauty of its color and the amazing juicy flavor as I bit into it. I made a piece of toast, slathered it with salted butter, and turned the buttery side towards my tongue, so I could really taste it. Then I made a cup of cocoa made with cacao, local honey, and grass-fed whole milk (I'm a fan of happy bees and happy cows, so investing in grass-fed dairy and local honey increases my pleasure). I made my bed so it looked visually appealing (another pleasure). I noticed my back was a little sore, so I did a calf stretch and psoas release (thank you, Larissa Parson) before settling in to write. Ahhhhhh. So good.

And now here you are reading this book. It's a product. It has been produced. And I enjoyed the process. No, not every minute of it. In fact, the day after I wrote this draft, I hit a bit of a wall emotionally, and after some rest, I leaned in on my ability to just keep putting one foot in front of the other. But overall, this book has been powered by pleasure and produced by my choice to flow with what shows up rather than pushing against it.

Just in case you need more motivation to try the path of pleasure, I want to add that claiming your sensual (and, yes, sexual) pleasure matters in the social justice world for other reasons too. The way sex, especially women's sexuality and the sexuality of LGBTQIA+ individuals has been portrayed and suppressed has been an incredibly effective tool in service of systemic oppression. It keeps anyone who isn't a cisgender, heterosexual male at risk, afraid, and often cut off from an incredible source of power and creativity — our sexual energy.

Finally, I'm acutely aware that most of you reading will rarely, if ever, have the ability to spend as much time in pleasure as I did in order to power up your workday (though you never know!). But you don't need a whole morning to start fueling your work through pleasure and turning down the dial on pushing harder as the only way to produce results. Up next: Tamara Robinson will inspire you to start adding pleasure into your daily routine bit by bit, so you have the fuel you need to go out and change the world.

PLEASURE: THE FUEL WE NEED TO THRIVE AND PURSUE OUR PASSIONS AND DREAMS

TAMARA ROBINSON

Author bio: Tamara Robinson is a passion and pleasure coach who helps women navigate the very real feelings of overwhelm and pain experienced after a heartbreak or a major life event. She's a mother, author, and poet who's enthusiastic about a daily existence of pleasure, flow, ease. Tamara's mission is to help women reclaim their sexual pleasure, have more confidence, and create more passion and pleasure in their lives.

Oftentimes, our bodies and souls let us down as we pursue our passions and dreams because we lack enough energy to push forward and stay focused. Our body is just like a car that won't function properly without enough fuel. This explains why some people with big dreams have trouble getting out of bed or accomplishing their daily goals. If you are struggling with this issue, you're not alone. I can relate.

As a busy working mom there was a time I was so stressed & overwhelmed with life that I often experienced feelings of burnout. I thought this was normal and something all moms experienced. When I became a single mom, after a 10-year marriage ended in divorce, I had to learn how to put the pieces of my life back together.

I soon began a daily meditation practice to connect more with my body and emotions. Self-care became a priority as I learned the importance of placing myself at the top of my daily list of priorities. I returned to my love of dance and enrolled in pole dance fitness classes at a local wellness center for women. Not only did those classes reconnect me with my love of dance, but I also gained confidence in my femininity, sensuality, and pleasure. This was the first time I viewed pleasure as the fuel I needed to thrive.

Let me show you how adding pleasure practices to your daily routine could help soothe your nerves and fill you with the energy and excitement that move you from surviving to thriving.

What is a pleasure practice?

Pleasure practices are activities done regularly to explore and enjoy pleasure, not unlike other practices that you do for your health like meditation or exercise. There are plenty of non-sex related pleasure practices: Bubble baths, naps, meditation, yoga, journaling, taking a dance class, listening to music, or enjoying a glass of wine (or water in a fancy wine glass)! There are also a variety of ways to experience sexual pleasure with or without a partner. These include breast massage, sensual rubbing and caressing your skin, touching sensual parts of your body, and self-pleasure (aka masturbation).

Some of these practices can be combined to increase your pleasurable experience. Add sensual music to an intimate moment by yourself, or with a significant other, and it can send you to a paradise of endless fun and fantasies! Try a few to see what works best for you.

Why add pleasure practices to your daily routine?

Pleasure practices are a means through which our body connects with our spirit and feels into the juicy sensations we're creating. Perhaps you've experienced the way that getting an orgasm through sexual pleasure can improve your sense of self-love, self-confidence, and self-esteem. I know in my life, as I've found that my body is a source of energy and delight that I can access, it connects me to a sense of abundance, proving my worth to myself and providing me with the motivation and confidence to pursue my dreams.

In my work with clients, I've noticed that stress is a major drawback that prevents them from pursuing their goals or remaining in the flow of creativity. Pleasure practices help them to focus on what they're feeling in the body rather than thinking about anything else. So, it allows them to let go of whatever is stressing them out.

Ultimately, the feeling that comes with pleasure practice fills you with the happy hormones and energy you need to achieve your dream. You can't pour from an empty cup! In my experience, making time for daily pleasure practices fills me with enough energy that I can give to others without being depleted myself. I invite you to add pleasure practices to your daily routine and see how it helps you to positively impact the world and accomplish your daily goals!

RESOURCES FOR YOUR JOURNEY

A Community Connection

Tamara Robinson is on Instagram @passionpleasurecoach where she shares pleasure-based sex and intimacy tips to help you reconnect to your desires and your sexual pleasure so you can move from Overwhelm to Orgasm. Her website is www.-passionpleasurecoach.com.

Practices to Try

1) Power up through pleasure.

Take a look at your calendar or your "to-do" list. Find something that you are committed to doing that you expect to be a challenge for you. Maybe you have a big board meeting coming up. Maybe it's a kid's birthday party. Instead of blocking out all the time you can to do the work of preparation, try blocking out some time for pleasure as PART of how you prepare. Journal about the experience.

. . .

2) Tiny extravagant joy object.

I am very picky about my mugs. The feel of the mug in my hand matters to me. It enhances my pleasure. The appearance of the mug matters less than the feel, but when both come together — like they did in the form of a pink, floral, perfectly-shaped, thermal mug that cost "too much," but that I bought anyway? It's a delight every time I use it. Extravagant, available joy. Joy that doesn't require that I have the exact work life I want, or a body of water nearby — though that is very, very nice when it happens. I wonder: What tiny, extravagant joy object have you been denying yourself that is actually within reach? A fuzzy pillow? A fabulous-smelling lotion? A chocolate truffle? Fresh flowers? No matter what your budget, you likely have a couple of dollars that you make choices about each week. And yes, in this case I'm suggesting that you spend money on yourself, because most of the people I work with have all kinds of resistance to doing just that. If it's not your thing, no worries, skip it. These exercises are always an invitation, not a requirement! If you try it, notice whether adding this tiny bit of pleasure to your life helps or hurts your big work in the world.

3) Prioritize sexual pleasure — with and without your partner(s) if you have one.

If that feels challenging for you, connect with a coach like Tamara for support, or check out the book *Come As You Are* by Emily Nagotski for a DIY start. Again, notice, when you enjoy some sexual pleasure what happens to your energy levels? Does it help or hinder your big work?

4) If your daily work is more misery, stress, and striving than pleasure, return to the time/joy diary from Chapter 1.

Start to follow your joy. Step-by-step. You are meant to spread your radiance and heal the world. I'm 100 percent sure of that. With pleasure and joy as guides, you'll find your way.

BOOKS

Pleasure Activism by adrienne maree brown. I'll admit, some of the explorations of this book go a bit beyond my comfort zone, but that's part of what I like about it. Plus, it's pleasure and activism together in one book. How's that for *Feel Better. Do Better?*

Book of Delights by Ross Gay. One thing I love about this delightful book is its size. Like my mugs, it feels good in my hand. Even better, I love how Ross Gay finds delight in sorrow and struggles, not in a spiritual bypassing kind of way, but more like how a weaver makes beauty from many colors of thread.

6

ALTERNATIVES TO CANCEL CULTURE:
BOUNDARIES, COMPASSION, AND
RECLAIMING CONNECTION

This chapter is an invitation to shift from habits of obligation, judgment, and exile as strategies for moving towards justice and healing to habits of empowered choice, compassion, and connection. Of course, there could be whole books written on any one of these subjects, but I'd at least like to get you started.

1) Letting go of obligation as a way to get things done: Let's create cultures where we express, support, and respect each others' "nos."

There is a both/and with "nos." We need to learn to say them for ourselves, and we need to respect them when they come from others. Women can be particularly challenged in saying — and accepting — empowered "nos" because we have often been socialized to "be nice" and to expect "nice" from others. But I'd like you to notice that on the flip side of a "yes" that wanted to be a "no" lie resentment, exhaustion, and often harsh judgment, making it virtually impossible for us to offer compassion to others when it's needed.

The need to set clear boundaries is crucial for people who are members of marginalized groups. I'm thinking especially of BIPOC folks here, but of course, there are others. It's likely that you will regularly need to refuse to accept a role that has been given to you without your consent — often that of educator or comforter of White folks, or road-paver and example for everyone else who looks like you. Just because you are "the only one" in the room, because someone expects you to respond or may be offended when you don't, doesn't mean that you must say yes.

I've found that many White people working in racial justice circles also need to learn to say no. While we might acknowledge that BIPOC people can say no sometimes, we believe we can't. For me, learning that I, too, have a responsibility to check in with my inner wisdom before determining whether or how to engage in a particular action — and to say "no" when it isn't aligned with my truth — has actually led me to say a lot more "yeses." I've learned to take action in creative and courageous ways that are uniquely aligned with who I am. For White readers who are concerned that you'll say "no" too often, community accountability is the best answer I know to that concern. See Chapter 8.

For BIPOC readers who may think, "Of course, you can say no, White people refuse to do this work all the time." I hear you, and I know that's true. Allowing for the possibility of a "no" isn't the end of the story. We also need to increase our capacity to do hard things — which I find to be a particularly common need among sensitive spiritual types and White women — we'll talk about this in the next chapter.

. . .

2) Letting go of judgment as a motivator for change: Let's lean into compassion and understanding.

Remember back in Chapter 2, you were invited to consider the possibility that you're already good and to start practicing self-compassion? Well, please don't let that go because you'll need it as we continue down this path.

I now want to invite you to lean into a practice of holding compassion for people with whom you strongly disagree. I don't just have an intellectual commitment to compassion. I have a felt sense of its power to transform from the inside out. I've been on the receiving and the giving end of compassion while working for racial healing and justice.

Receiving compassion can be challenging — often because we're judging ourselves internally and because being the receiver is a place of vulnerability. I, for example, have at times been unwilling (or unable) to receive compassion offered to me by BIPOC colleagues who have chosen to be in relationship with me and are offering it freely. I've had to practice putting down what I sometimes call my "shame shield" and respecting their right to love and trust me if they want to!

Largely due to a training on how to have difficult conversations about racism based on the method Dr. Amanda Kemp created, I've also practiced leaning into compassionate understanding as a way to approach conversations about race — both in my family and in professional settings. I now approach conversations about racism and other charged topics with the intention of holding onto and speaking my truth and seeking to understand theirs. I ask questions to try to understand their point of view. I focus on sharing personal stories rather than showering others with a barrage of fact-weapons designed to defeat and defend. Conversations with family members have been much more effective than when it was all intellectual attack and defense — or hiding and avoidance. And there have even been some significant changes in a coaching community I'm part of because I was able to show up with courage and compassion.

Honestly, I'll never cease to be amazed that BIPOC people like those who have contributed to this book choose to work in interracial spaces, given all they have carried and still carry. I have seen many times over the power that the compassionate, honest, and courageous presence of colleagues like these brings to charged situations and how it opens doors to new ways forward that otherwise would have slammed shut. Compassion isn't easy, but it is effective.

3) Letting go of exile as a strategy for justice. Let's acknowledge connection and create paths to redemption.

I want to put forth the possibility that naming particular individuals as evil and exiling them (or excommunicating them, or excluding them) doesn't solve anything. There are a number of problems with this approach, from my view, but one of them is that it allows us to think that our work is done. We see a horrible wrong. We call an individual bad. We exile them in some way — whether that is off the girls' basketball court, off their TV show, out of school, out of their job, or into prison. We wipe our hands of the whole situation. All done. Solved. But it's not solved.

Calling a person evil and exiling them just puts them out of our line of vision. We don't have to see their humanness. We don't have to see how they are like us. We don't have to address the systems, structures, and beliefs that led to their actions — and the ways we are complicit. It supports the fictional story we want to tell that says we're off the hook. But until we are "on the hook" together, we're not going to move forward towards healing and justice.

The second reason that I'd like to invite us to stop supporting exile as a strategy for justice is that it usually leaves the offender with virtually no way to move forward. There's no path of redemption; there's no way back into community. No wonder people are terrified to admit when they've made a mistake because the threat of being labeled as "racist," "homophobic," "sexist," or "a criminal" is akin to the threat of death. Because as humans, we're made for connection.[1]

I'm not saying that no one should be fired or expelled or otherwise removed from situations where they are doing harm until they can do better, but there are examples of ways to move forward that offer the possibility of redemption, healing, and repair. The Corrymeela Community in Ireland, and restorative justice initiatives in schools, are great examples. And perhaps next will be the amazing community healing process *you* will help to create when you decide you're ready to step into your power!

Kristen's story below is very different from mine, as is her racial and ethnic heritage, but we have a shared commitment to the messy, often uncomfortable process of learning to love and offer compassion across categories of difference that could be barriers to connection. In the following essay, she invites readers who are People of Culture to claim their culture and heritage in the ways that work for them — saying no to what doesn't resonate, having compassion for the ways you might have rejected parts of yourself in order to survive, and reconnecting in the ways that you desire to now.

RECLAIMING YOU THROUGH CULTURE AND HERITAGE

KRISTEN MUN

Author bio: Kristen Mun was born and raised on the island of Oahu. She currently lives in Portland, Oregon, where she works as a cultural consultant, racial justice facilitator, and a core member of the Accountability Collective, a group of volunteers working toward racial equality for the Portland theatre community. When she is not a facilitator and project manager with Racial Justice from the HEART she is a stage manager and fight choreographer in the Portland theatre community.

This essay is for the People of Culture out there who are proud of their race and heritage, but find it hard to express that pride. This essay is for people of mixed descent who are trying to find their way in both worlds. And this essay is for the people who love them and want to support that journey wherever it takes them.

First, I want to share a bit of my own journey. Early in my experience of working professionally in the field of racial justice, I was practicing for an implicit bias workshop with my mentor. After the presentation my mentor looked at me and said, "Kristen, you did great, but I'm gonna say something to you and I want you to think about it. You never mention race in your whole presentation. The woman being interviewed is Taiwanese and that is important to her. It is how she identifies, but you didn't mention it. You never mentioned your own race either. Why do you think that is?"

I paused and thought deeply about this question. Why did I avoid talking about race? Specifically, why did I avoid talking about MY race?

As I continued my work and continued to have conversations about race and racism in my community, I found I was not the only one. Many of my friends identified with my actions. They also felt confused and embarrassed that they avoided talking about race. It's not that we weren't proud Asians or Mexicans or Iranians, etc. What was preventing us from claiming our racial identities?

When you are a Person of the Culture working and living in primarily White spaces, you find ways to "fit in" and be accepted. In some ways you are rewarded for adopting White culture; you become "one of us." The more you let go of your culture, the more you fit in.

But if you lead with your ethnicity and show pride in being different, you are likely to find yourself constantly educating White folks on your own culture, or on why you don't know about another culture or group (for example: All Asians are not all the same OR just because I am Chinese does not mean I know everything about China). The microaggressions and subtle racism start to compound and can be overwhelming, so you just adapt to survive.

But what happens to us when we deny our culture? When we ignore our race? What happens to our identity?

I have a friend who is from India who works as a film and television actor. When I told my story about how I adapted to White American culture to the point that I lost myself, he shared his. When he first started school in the States, he had a thick Indian accent and was embarrassed of it. He worked hard to get rid of it. By the time he graduated his Indian accent was gone. At the time he wore it like a badge of honor and pride. "I did it! I can fit in now." Losing his accent meant that he felt more comfortable in White spaces; he felt safe. "Now though," he said to me, "it feels like a loss. Like I lost a part of myself."

For me, I realized that I had ignored my race because I felt ashamed. "I wasn't Asian enough," but also, "I wasn't American enough." This discovery caused me to start down a different path, one in which I intentionally cultivated pride in my racial and ethnic identities, in the midst of a culture that still tells me that they aren't of value.

For the People of Culture out there, this is a reminder that you are perfect the way you are.

It's very likely that you are a product of an environment that rewarded you for fitting in. You don't need to feel ashamed for doing so. And I want you to know that anything you feel like you lost is not gone forever; it is and always will be a part of you. Reclaim the things that you identify with, but don't adopt things to fit a stereotype if it does not feel true to you.

Here are some things that I have done to reclaim my heritage and my culture that you may want to try:

- Follow an artist of your identity/ heritage; buy their art! Put it on your walls.
- Find music that affirms you.
- Learn about your family history, and keep your heart and mind open.
- Lean in to your culture and race — read books, learn more stories.
- Join an affinity group or space (see Joyce's essay in Chapter 8 for more about this).
- And most importantly, be truthful and kind to yourself.

Your journey is not wrong or a mistake, your journey is your own and it is what makes you, you. Confront the uncomfortable truths and, in the end, you will find more of yourself than you started out with.

RESOURCES FOR YOUR JOURNEY

A Community Connection

Want to connect with some like-minded folks who are creating community across racial divides?

Head over to dramandakemp.com and find out what's going on there. You're likely to run into Kristen there.

Practices to Try

1) Break a rule (a practice in letting go of obligation).

This practice was inspired by the eccentric octogenarian Iris Apfel who stated in the Netflix documentary about her, "I don't have any rules because I'd always be breaking them. So, it's a waste of time." Just writing that statement makes me so happy! It's the freedom to choose *and* not apologize for it. Those of us who live our lives according to the "shoulds" of obligation need to practice our way to that kind of freedom. So, here's my challenge: Break a rule.

· · ·

It could be tiny.

- Say no to one holiday tradition that you've always hated.
- Buy yourself the expensive lotion you love even though you were taught be frugal.
- Wear an item of clothing that is "inappropriate" for your age or your body.

It could be bigger.

- Take a stand at work when you've always followed the mandate to "support the institution".
- Admit to your family that you are gay/trans/not Christian/not vegan — whatever it is that is key to your identity, but breaks the family rules.
- Participate in civil disobedience.
- Live where you want to live.

2) Pass the baton — A special "let go of obligation" exercise for BIPOC folx: Ask one of your White friends to get themselves together and proactively talk to their people.

Also ask if you can send people their way when you get approached AGAIN. We really do need to do our own work now, but as a group we are masters at avoidance. My hunch is that the White people who know and love you will likely say yes to your direct ask. It just might be the nudge they need to get out there. NOTE: this practice can be adapted for anyone with an identity that is the target of oppression who is often called on to educate or challenge people in the privileged group.

3) Set an intention to build a bridge of understanding — A practice for anyone who wants to lean-in with compassion and connection, instead of judgment and exile.

Caveat: I can't know FOR YOU whether you are called to build bridges — especially if you'd be doing so with people who are in a group that has historically caused you harm. But some of us know that we COULD build bridges — if we tried. It's just that we don't want to. If that's you, consider me your cheerleader. We need you. You can do this!

This practice isn't a one-and-done deal. It's an invitation to make a commitment to increase your capacity to offer love and understanding across painful divides, until this new way of being dominates your life.

It concerns me that the liberal left — those of us who believe ourselves to be more tolerant, enlightened, and progressive; who operate in circles where mindfulness and compassion and empathy are buzzwords — typically aren't willing (or able) to listen to people we've deemed to be on the wrong side of justice. We want them to listen to us, though.

We expect them to set aside their strong emotions and deep beliefs — often associated with their personal interpretations of painful life experiences — in an instant or we will call them evil, backward, and treat them as barely worthy of existence.

My question is this. Will you commit to learning how to set aside YOUR strong emotions, deep beliefs, and painful memories long enough to listen to their stories? In order to be a leader in healing? In order to bring more justice? Will you grapple with the problem of your intolerance of people who aren't tolerant? Will you find the support you need to be able to invite them to your table? If you're a yes, let me know and I'll gladly share some other resources that might help you get started. You can find me at debshine@thriving4equity.com.

A BOOK AND MORE

Inclusive Conversations by Mary-Frances Winters.

The book itself is a great support, but you don't have to stop there. Go to https://www.wintersgroup.com/live-inclusively/ and make the commitment to live inclusively. It's powerful!

7

THE PATH OF DOING BETTER IS LEARNABLE — YOU HAVE THE POWER TO CHOOSE IT

This chapter is for those of you who are stuck mostly *not* doing the work you want to do in the world. It's also for those who feel guilty because you believe you should be doing more or better but can't imagine how.

I have so much good news for you. Really. I can pretty much guarantee that you can make the kind of impact you want to make in the world. I'm not saying that releasing that power is just one affirmation away — though affirmations can be supportive at times. But I *am* saying that you can access it, or perhaps more accurately, you can release it. That's one of the best things about being human. You. Can. Learn. Here are some examples.

You may think you're not courageous enough to stand up for justice. Maybe not now, but you can strengthen your courage muscles and learn how to care for the parts that are afraid.

You may think you're not disciplined enough to care for your body in ways that would give you the energy you need to keep showing up. There are ways to make lasting change and to do so with ease, in partnership with your body instead of battling against it.

You may think you're too emotionally sensitive, too emotionally reactive, or too screwed up and broken from your fucked-up childhood to ever be able to truly shine. Not possible, though you will need to allow some space for healing and get some support.

You may have big dreams you've given up on because every time you try to move towards them, you realize that you don't know how to get there. So, you let them go. I've got news for you: You're not supposed to know the "how" before you start. You will learn as you go. That's how life works.

You may stop yourself from even trying to be an advocate or an ally because you're so afraid of screwing up. You will. And you'll learn from it and do better the next time.

And for those of you who are great at achieving and powering through but are missing the sense of delight you used to have in being alive. You can learn how to create a life, and a world, in which that wonderlight in your heart shines as brightly as your gold stars. Or brighter. And the work you create from that place will be so much more powerful than you can imagine right now.

Here are a few examples of what you can learn.

- To genuinely love your body, stop judging it — or endlessly improving it — so you can use your energy for things that matter.
- How to have difficult and effective conversations about racism without falling apart.

- To find your partner's body attractive again, so you can connect in ways that support both of you to do what you're called to do.
- How to ride the wave of difficult emotions, so they energize your work instead of sidelining you.
- To be near to and with suffering people without losing connection with the joy of life.
- How to decrease your unconscious biases so you do less harm.
- About the history of the land you live on and ways to honor that history.
- How to let go of traumas that are held in your body.
- How to discern what's your work to do and say no to what isn't, so you make your unique contribution, your way and avoid burning out.
- How to make more money so you feel more abundantly supported (and can spoil people you love and support causes you care about).
- To speak out and speak up even though you've always been terribly shy.
- To respect other people's empowered "nos" without feeling hurt and rejected.
- To let go of guilt and shame, so you can focus your energy on doing what you are made to do.

Each of the above items is something I have learned that I didn't know I could. I could go on, but you get the idea.

I'm not saying you have to, need to, or will learn the same things I did. But what I am saying is that if you are stuck and exhausted, you have some stories that you tell yourself — about who you are and who you will always be — that don't have to continue to be true. You have beliefs that don't help you to do better work in the world. And you can choose to change them. You might need a little help to see new possibilities, but you can learn.

There are tiny steps you could take RIGHT now that you're not taking because you follow your mind off into the land of perfectionism, comparison, and overwhelm instead. You don't have to "up the ante" deciding that what you can do now isn't enough. You can just do your tiny little thing. And then the next one. You can grow your capacity, knowledge, and skill.

As verbal land acknowledgments have become more commonplace, I found myself once again wanting to "get it right" in relation to Indigenous peoples but not knowing how. Jennifer Folayan was one of the people who graciously called me in around this issue, not allowing me to throw a quick statement up to make myself feel better and not giving me the answers but inviting me into a process of learning.

As you read her essay, I hope you will not only say yes to her invitation to be part of a collective journey towards healing and connection with Indigenous communities (if you aren't Indigenous yourself) but that you will see it as an example of what is possible when you decide to learn what you need to learn to increase your capacity to do your part of the healing work that's needed. Not all the parts. Not parts you're not ready for yet, but your part. And to keep learning so that down the road, you have the capacity for more.

LAND ACKNOWLEDGMENTS AND OTHER STEPS TOWARDS HEALING AND CONNECTION WITH INDIGENOUS COMMUNITIES

JENNIFER FOLAYAN

Author bio: Jennifer Folayan is a Maryland business owner, artist, and graphic designer. She has created programs to empower and unite survivors of rape, incest, domestic violence, and foster care youth through healing arts. She is of Pueblo, Cherokee, Aztec, and Spanish descent and serves on the Board of Directors for the Baltimore American Indian Center. She is an active peer-to-peer mentor for the National Alliance on Mental Illness. Jennifer believes each person has the potential to create a life filled with happiness and love.

"When we talk about land, land is part of who we are.
It's a mixture of our blood, our past, our current, and our
future. We carry our ancestors in us, and they're around us.
As you all do."

Mary Lyons (Leech Lake Band of Ojibwe)[1]

My name is Jennifer Folayan, and I am the daughter of Patsy (Gonzales) Chaine and George Terry Anthony (Marquez) Chaine. I am the granddaughter of ancestors from California and New Mexico. We are Pueblo, Cherokee, Spanish, Irish, French, and Indigenous.

I serve on the board of the Baltimore American Indian Center, and I am a key community organizer with Indigenous Strong, a grassroots organization that advocated for and passed Indigenous Peoples Day for the City of Baltimore in 2021. Yes, Indigenous folks are still here!

Land acknowledgments serve to recognize the lands of the Indigenous communities that exist and have existed for centuries before colonization. As an Indigenous woman, when land is acknowledged in public spaces, I feel visible and recognized. It's a small step towards healing and acknowledging we are here and have been erased. Land acknowledgments should be given by the allies as a practice of reconciliation. Indigenous people should not be constantly asked to give the acknowledgement.

Land acknowledgment is complicated. The United States and Canadian governments displaced many Tribes from lands before treaties were signed. Many policies forced Indigenous children into boarding and residential schools to, "Kill the Indian and Save the Man." We should not sugarcoat the past. Terms like genocide, ethnic cleansing, stolen land, and forced removal may be used to reflect actions taken by colonizers.

Beyond just adding a land acknowledgement to your email signature, how can you be an ally? The key at the end of the day is connection. Here are some steps you might take:

Do research to learn the tribes of your area — past and present.

Attend a public powwow or celebration. Make sure you check to see what guidelines are in place for attendance.

Volunteer with or donate to local organizations that support Indigenous peoples, especially those who are active with MMIWG (Missing and Murdered Indigenous Women and Girls) and those supporting residential school survivors.

Write to your local officials and advocate to abolish Columbus Day and celebrate Indigenous Peoples' Day as an official holiday.

Connecting to the Earth is another way to honor to Indigenous ways of interacting with the land and each other. Look up the Haudenosaunee Thanksgiving address. Use this greeting to the natural world as a guide. Take a moment to go outside and find a favorite tree, or a spot in nature to sit. Take a deep breath and look around. Breathe deeply and ask for any ancestors to join you. Become aware of sights, sounds, how the air feels, and of any fragrances. Read the Thanksgiving address and pause as you acknowledge the natural world.

I thank you for the journey you are on. You have a beautiful light to discover and shine. I invite you to make space each day to tune in to your best self and allow the voices of the land and our ancestors to guide you.

Now our minds and hearts are one.

RESOURCES FOR YOUR JOURNEY

A Community Connection

If you'd like to connect with Jennifer, you can email her at jfolayan@gmail.com or find her on Facebook!

Practices to Try

1) Follow one or more of Jennifer's suggestions above.

2) Do the Google step — "It's easy to gain more knowledge by doing your own research."

This practice is rooted in an "ah-ha" moment in a training I participated in.[1] The focus of the training was to help cisgender heterosexuals to first assess and then increase our capacity to provide a "safe enough" container for LGBTQIA+ folks who come to us as clients. "Safe enough" because as humans we can never be perfect and because transformative work always requires that we step into new territory that may not always feel totally safe (as in, "comfortable for our nervous systems"). One of the points made by the workshop facilitator was that coaches who don't identify as LGBTQIA+ should have a baseline level of knowledge about the LGBTQIA+ experience. We should know some common language or terms used such as "passing" or "butch," for example. We should know key leaders, historical moments of importance, and important role models. We should learn about some of the common experiences LGBTQIA+ people have often or typically. Then the facilitator said this: "It's easy to gain more knowledge by doing your own research."

OH. MY. GOSH. That simple sentence hit me right in the gut, in the most delightful way. Like when you can't help laughing at yourself — because you missed something that was right in front of your nose, or on your head (as is often the case for me when I'm looking for my glasses!)

It's so true — at least for people in my context, living with access to the internet and a smartphone. There are books, articles, movies, and podcasts that can help us to grow our knowledge instead of requiring our friends to educate us. It's easy for me to do something that could make someone else feel more seen, more understood, more safe, more loved. And it's easy for you. Where have you thought, "I wish I knew more about the experiences of X group of people," or, "I wish I knew how to help X group of people," or, " I wish I knew why X group is so angry." How about making a choice to follow that curiosity? I call it the "Google step." And it's easy to learn.

3) Increase your emotional strength by learning some new emotion words and starting to be more specific as you name what you're feeling.

Search for "emotion wheel" and you'll find plenty of options! Practice naming and feeling what you feel (see Chapter 4). Notice that you can.

4) When you are deeply hurting in response to recent events, especially if they involve people with whom you share a targeted identity, try these things:

- Feel what you feel. Grieve. Cry. Seek comfort. Don't soldier on and fight the fight right now. Scream. Rage. Find others who can hear you; don't bother for now with those who can't.
- Remember what you need when you feel deep anguish and make sure you get it. You probably need more than what you think is reasonable to need — more quiet, less action, more silence, less news, more time — not because you are avoiding the pain, or want to hide in a safe bubble, but because you already feel it ALL.
- It's your job to get what you need, so you can bring your strongest, most hopeful, most joyful, most whole self to the battle for love and healing.
- Look for the parts of yourself that you want to judge and reject. Start loving those seemingly ugly parts that seem like they don't deserve love. We can't send that kind of love and acceptance out into the world without starting with ourselves. And it's needed.

- Then act to bring love and light in whatever way you personally feel called to do, big or small — whether that is to care for your own body, to write a letter to the editor, or to head to a protest.

5) For White folks, and cisgendered heterosexual folks especially: Seek help, training, and support so that you can have hard, scary conversations about racism, sexism, homophobia and other biases and oppressions with family and friends and in organizations you're part of, so that people in these targeted groups don't have to (a bit of emotional reparations).

You will need help, support, and training. There are many places to find it. My recommendation is that you avoid trainings and groups that focus on shame (see Chapter 6) and seek spaces where you will be both challenged and loved as you learn. But do find what you need. You can learn. And it matters.

6) For any other area where you want to learn how to do better, start by imagining that it's possible.

Then take one step towards it. Make it tiny. Celebrate yourself.

PODCASTS

The Matriarch Movement, hosted by Shayla Oulette Stonechild, shares stories of Indigenous women from Canada, Turtle Island, and beyond.

More than Money with Jaquette Timmons — funny and fabulous info if one place where you need to be empowered is in your financial life.

8

NO LONE WOLVES: IF YOU'RE GOING TO WALK THIS PATH, DON'T GO IT ALONE

In this final chapter, I want to remind you of what you likely know in your head but might have trouble putting into practice. We all need ongoing connection and support to create sustainable and joyful ways to change the world for the better. Even helpers need help.

There are as many ways to seek and find human support and connection as there are humans. In relation to the topic of this book, I especially want to encourage you to seek relationships and spaces where:

- You will be met with compassion.
- You can tell and be told the truth without harsh judgment.
- You'll be encouraged to connect with your body and your inner wisdom.
- You can feel big feelings and others in the group will be with you, but not try to fix you.
- You aren't expected or encouraged to be a superhero or a savior.

- You can mess up and try again.

Let's start with the importance of putting yourself in groups, communities, and relationships where you will be challenged when you need it and reminded of the commitments you've made to keep moving forward. I love the metaphor that Beverly Daniel Tatum used in *Why Are All The Black Kids Sitting Together in the Cafeteria?* of racism as a moving sidewalk. She uses it to make the argument that if you're not actively walking against racism, you're moving with it. I think this metaphor works in relation to any of the oppressive, unhealthy systems we want to stop supporting. Going against societal norms takes focus and effort. And with everything else that calls for our attention, it can be easy not to notice that we're going with the flow, but not in a good way. We need people who will let us know when that's happening.

So, please, especially if you have many privileged identities, seek out people who will challenge you, who are willing to say the hard things. But that's not the end of the story. It's also essential that you seek and accept help (of course, sharing hard truths with you actually is a form of help, too.)

Accepting help is not always easy. Part of what the myth of the American Dream has done to us as a group is to cause us to equate needing help with moral failure. Even our charity programs are designed to ensure help only for the "worthy poor."[1]

But as anyone reading this likely doesn't need to be told, American individualism is a myth — we all need and get help along the way. In fact, the somewhat invisible help that privileged people get is a big part of what keeps systems of inequality in place. But, even if we know all this in our heads, being on the receiving end of help is not generally something we aspire to.

Here's an example from my own life. Recently, in a coaching session during which I was the client, not the coach, we hit a place in my interior world where I felt a strong presence of someone else's energy. Even if you don't use the word "energy" to describe it, you've probably had the experience of having someone else's voice in your head, often a negative one, exerting a powerful influence over your thoughts, feelings, and choices. My coach asked me where I wanted that energy to be, and I said I wanted it back with the person, in their house, their body. She asked if I was ready to set that boundary. I said yes. Then came the tricky question.

"Do you want or need help?" she asked.

I hesitated.

"It's okay to need and ask for help," she said.

I don't remember if I started to cry (there's usually a good bit of crying for me when I do this kind of work), but I do remember that I felt the impact of that permission. And it made me aware that part of me was trying to give the "more right" answer of, "No, I don't need help." We'd hit on a key code in my internal system. Even though I would tell you, and everyone, that asking for and needing help is just the way we're made to live as humans — interdependently — deep inside, I still believe that the MOST right way is to do it yourself.

You likely have different reasons than I do for not seeking help. Perhaps you've been let down too many times before.

You learned early that depending on others isn't safe. If you're a Black woman, for example, there's a lot of evidence that no one else will step up for you if you don't take care of business yourself. If you're a man, you've been taught from birth that you're supposed to be the provider, the one who protects, never the one who receives. If you haven't worked through the shame you carry about all your privileges, you may think that you don't deserve support because you've already gotten your fair share.

Because you're reading this book, I can pretty much guarantee that you have good reasons to stay solidly in "be the helper" mode. I get it. But if you want your work to be as powerful and sustainable as it's meant to be, I hope you'll stop trying to go it alone.

I want to offer you here what my coach offered me, not just permission, but an invitation to seek out and request the help, connection, and support that is always available to you — from your ancestors and from Nature/the Earth (as Jennifer suggested in Chapter 7), from the Universe/the Divine, from angels and other beings of unconditional love you're not even sure you believe in, just in case they exist. And especially from other humans — humans with whom you share many identities and humans with whom you don't.

The bonus of this collaborative approach to doing better work in the world is that the process also creates the "product" we so long for — a world in which all humans belong and all humans thrive. And I can say from experience it's way more interesting and FUN!

In the final contributor essay of this book, Joyce Washington tells us why she thinks affinity groups are of particular importance for Black people working for justice and equity. If you're in a marginalized or oppressed group seeking connection with others who share similar experiences, especially if you spend a lot of your time in spaces where you're in the minority, finding (or creating) an affinity group might be your next step on the path to feeling better and doing better work in the world.

WHY I BELIEVE IN AFFINITY GROUPS

JOYCE WASHINGTON

Author bio: Joyce Washington served as a catastrophe team leader for Allstate Corporation for 42 years. Now, a social justice advocate, her mission is to help eradicate systemic and institutional racism, representing people with "no voice." Joyce is a chairperson for the Weakley County Reconciliation Project (engaging communities in conversations about race) and for the Martin Housing Authority. She is a certified racial justice facilitator, Delta Sigma Theta Sorority member, and has three children and seven grandchildren.

My perspective on the value of affinity groups is developed from my work as a racial justice facilitator, often working in interracial settings, and as someone who spent over forty years in a predominately white institution. Through these experiences, it became clear that there is real value and a need for affinity groups for people of the global majority. This is especially true for Black people and specifically for Black women. I view affinity groups as a critical component of supporting self-care for people of color and racial justice.

Often, the idea of affinity spaces comes as an affront to White people who are either unable to understand the need or who feel hurt because they think that only "bad" White people should be excluded from these groups. If you're a White reader, I want to remind you that patterns of White dominance are ever-present in predominantly White spaces. As a facilitator, I hear Black and other global majority people express their frustrations and anger with not being seen, valued, or heard and constantly representing the entire culture while ensuring that the dominant culture is comfortable.

People of Color in integrated groups can often feel like we are swimming upstream. Characteristics of White supremacy culture, such as perfectionism, fear of open conflict, or a sense of urgency surface even among White people seeking to do the work to break the cycle of racial bias. In sharing our experiences, it is usually necessary to use language that allows White people to be sympathetic. When we share our experiences of racial harm or bias in these groups, we must defend our feelings and experiences. When judgment and insecurity surface in mixed groups, we often feel guilty and responsible and fall into the socialized role of comforting White people. This is frustrating, exhausting, and, more significantly, not our issue!

By contrast, affinity groups allow Black people and other people of the global majority our own spaces, where we can gather outside of the dominant environment's stereotypes and alienations. These spaces enable us to say aloud all we are experiencing and, most importantly, feeling. We can be seen and heard as our authentic selves without the judgment and insecurity of the dominant culture. We can share painful experiences of discrimination, microaggressions, and oppression without worrying about White listeners being defensive, uncomfortable, or shifting the focus. There is support, healing, and hope found in these spaces. Additionally, there is the opportunity to develop skills to push through to survive in integrated settings and truly thrive.

> James Baldwin said it best: "To be a Negro in this country and to be relatively conscious is to be in a state of rage almost, almost all of the time — and in one's work. And part of the rage is this: It isn't only what is happening to you. But it's what's happening all around you and all of the time in the face of the most extraordinary and criminal indifference, indifference of most white people in this country, and their ignorance."[1]

I can confirm that Baldwin's rage is absolute and has existed for hundreds of years. It manifests in our bodies in physical and emotional ways. Affinity groups are one way to release this rage and begin healing ourselves.

If you are a Black person or in another oppressed and marginalized group, I encourage you to actively seek out others of like mind and perspective and find (or form) an affinity group. If you are a White person on your journey for racial justice, one of the ways you can support the cause is to notice and seek support for yourself among like-minded White people on the journey to social justice. I also invite you to help others of the dominant culture embrace and understand the experiences of Black people and others of the global majority and the need for affinity spaces as part of our journey towards racial justice and healing.

RESOURCES FOR YOUR JOURNEY

A Community Connection

Reach out to Joyce at joyce.washington@jmwconsulting.net for inspiration, self-care, coaching, and support in raising your awareness and energy as you continue on your journey towards racial justice, equality, and inclusion.

Practices to Try

1) Read the "Declaration of Interdependence" by Richard Blanco in his book *How to Love a Country* (or google it — you can find it online as well) and work on memorizing it with me, so it sinks into our bones and blood and heart just like the poisons of White supremacy and sexism and classism and all the other messed up stuff has. I want some new medicine to take up space in me. I find poetry can help.

2) Connect with family members or close friends and see if they're up for doing some reading (or listening to a podcast or other series), talking, and growing together in one of the areas where you both need and desire to learn.

For example, the *Scene on Radio* podcast[1] has several series that take on various aspects of oppression.

3) When you find you're having trouble following through on something you want to do, ask someone to be an accountability buddy.

For example, I just wrapped up several weeks of daily texts with a friend who joyfully helped me to show up for a daily movement practice that I love doing, but avoid anyway. And I currently have a weekly phone chat with another writer to keep us both moving forward.

4) Create ongoing commitment buddies.

For example, in relation to my commitment to work for racial justice and healing, I have an agreement with a couple White friends that we can call each other as needed for processing and support. And a six-week-long group that met to do the practices from *My Grandmother's Hands* was a crucial source of support for me recently when I took a stand in an organization I'm part of where unconscious racial bias had shown up. My mind knew I was not in danger, but my body felt terror as I spoke up. The group helped me prepare myself for the conversation and process it afterwards.

5) As Joyce said, and as Dave described in his story, for BIPOC people, whether actively doing racial justice work or not, finding places to be where you're not under the "White gaze" is crucial and deserved.

And, again, that goes for people with other oppressed identities as well, particularly trans and non-binary people who have been under new waves of attack globally and in the U.S.

6) Consider investing in paid support as well.

Find a therapist or coach that is a good fit for you, or join a group program. If you're new to the therapy/coaching world, I suggest looking for key terms like "somatic" or "embodied practices" in how they describe themselves. I've also found therapists trained in Internal Family Systems therapy to be very supportive. We all have trauma of some kind, so even if you aren't aware of any "Big T" trauma in your life, I recommend looking for trauma-informed coaches and healers wherever you go. I'm one of them. So is Tamara. And trust yourself — if you meet with someone and it doesn't feel like a good fit, look elsewhere.

7) Each of the contributors to this book offers support of different kinds, paid and unpaid.

If you haven't explored the options yet, you could start there!

Therapy for Black Girls — a weekly conversation with licensed psychologist Dr. Joy Harden Bradford exploring "mental health, personal development, and all the small decisions we can make to become the best possible version of ourselves."

Finding Our Way with healer, teacher, and Somatics practitioner Prentis Hemphill — it's "an exploration into ourselves, and the skills we need to create and embody the world we want."

CLOSURE

Well, we've reached the end of the invitations for now. I hope you've said a few "yeses" and found a few new possibilities. I hope you feel a glimmer of your inner radiance shining through. I hope you feel just a tiny bit more loved and loving. I hope that you feel the possibility of thriving for equity.

You can feel better and still be a good person. In fact, I believe the path to your joy, health, and vitality is also the path to your most creative and impactful work in the world. But don't take my word for it, try it and see.

If you read through the book quickly and are feeling over-whelmed, I encourage you to choose just one practice to try. Choose the one you're most curious about. Or the one that you think is the most ridiculous — why not?! There's no way to do it wrong. If you feel the need to try two, make the second one celebrating yourself for doing the first one. You are so worth celebrating.

Have questions or comments? I'd love to hear from you. Email me at debshine@thriving4equity.com.

TEACHERS, MENTORS, AND TRAININGS

Virtually all of what I share in this book has been influenced by these teachers and trainings. Some ideas — like understanding the inner critic, limiting beliefs, an invitation to listen to the body, and viewing emotions and intuition as valid sources of wisdom — were core aspects of multiple trainings. I have referenced specific teachers and programs in the book where I draw on an idea that is directly connected to that body of knowledge.

Katherine North of declaredominion.com

Katherine is a dear friend and my first coach. Her Queen Sweep program helped me to learn to do daily things that opened up space for more beauty and joy in my life. It was with her that I first learned the power of practicing celebration — for tiny steps which she called "wee brags." It was while working with her that I created the time/joy diary. She provided my first introduction to the idea that changing what I say and think could change what I felt. She helped me interpret important messages from my dreams and opened me up to the possibility that life could be challenging and also delightful — and that I could hold all of it.

Dr. Amanda Kemp and the Racial Justice From the Heart (RJFTH) Facilitators Training

I met three of the contributing authors — Kristen (Chapter 6), Jennifer (Chapter 7), and Joyce (Chapter 8) — when I was training to be a Racial Justice from the Heart Facilitator in the summer of 2021. Created by Dr. Amanda Kemp, this approach to moving towards racial justice is grounded in mindfulness, self-compassion, and compassion for others. The team is inter-racial and inter-generational. Trainings are offered to mixed groups of participants who are both BIPOC and White, with the option of BIPOC-only small groups for those who want them. Amanda and her team have been an integral part in my journey to heal shame and increase my capacity for receiving and giving compassion while doing in the work of racial healing and justice.

Ijumaa Jordan

During my time as an early childhood education administrator at a large university, I worked with Ijumaa Jordan to address racial bias in myself and my department. She challenged me to see what was true and she refused to save me from the messiness of the process. She also supported and celebrated me when I took actions that scared my good-little-White-girl self to death. Through her I came to understand structural racism and to see my participation in it. I also increased my capacity and courage to act for equity and justice without giving into patterns of condemnation and judgment.

Tara Mohr and the Playing Big Facilitators Training

As a start for my own empowerment, the Playing Big training was essential. I consistently make use of almost every part of the framework presented in the training and in the book *Playing Big.* Especially influential have been ideas of "making it easy" as an alternative to "discipline," viewing criticism and praise as information about the speaker rather than yourself, the ways that good student habits often undermine success, especially for women, and the idea that we never know how to do what we're called to do when we start out towards it.

Martha Beck and the Wayfinder Life Coach Training

Martha Beck's life coach training was foundational for me, as were almost all of her books. Through her I first learned how to hear my body's "yes" and "no" and started regularly asking my clients to become body parts that seemed to have something to say, as a way to find out what they needed or longed for. It's also through this training that I learned Byron Katie's *The Work* as a means of opening new possibilities by changing thoughts.

Rochelle Schiek and Qoya Teacher Training

Qoya is a movement practice based on the idea that through movement we remember that our essence is wise, wild, and free. Best of all, there's no way to do it wrong. It integrates spirituality and movement and the community that has gathered around the practice has been an incredible gift to me. I've also been influenced by Rochelle's commitment to the messy journey of becoming more racially aware as a White woman and leader seeking to create a culture in which all bodies feel safe and welcome.

Makenna Held, Leadership Recipe and Future Writing®

Facilitators Training

I met Makenna Held in 2019 in France at an event she led with colleagues Andréa Ranae and Monica Prince. I've been working with her ever since. A White, queer woman, Makenna is intentional about acknowledging privilege and taking real action to equal the playing field. It's through Makenna that I learned that sexuality and spirituality and leadership are linked, which took me down the path of learning more. She helped me strengthen my boundaries and take radical responsibility for my life. She taught me what it meant to be radically committed to consent in marketing. And she's helped Dave and me to heal our financial lives.

Layla Martin and the VITA™ Sex, Love, and Relationship Coach Training

Another transformative program — I joined this one because I knew that my very conservative training around sex and sexuality, and the blocks it left in my body, were keeping me from accessing the pleasure, delight, and power available to me — and that many of my clients had similar challenges. Coming after my other coach trainings, this one brought in missing pieces around emotional empowerment, as well as sex and relationships.

Academic Life Coaching (ALC), a program of Coach Training EDU

ALC was the coach training I participated in. Though I don't use many of the specific tools I learned there now, it provided me with an understanding of ideas like the inner critic, inner mentor, and ways that our beliefs can change our interpretation of events.

ACKNOWLEDGMENTS

I am incredibly grateful to the eight contributing authors who said yes to this project without hesitation — Larissa, Trevia, Marquita, Dave, Tamara, Jennifer, Kristen, and Joyce. Without you this book wouldn't be what it's meant to be, and neither would I. I'm so grateful to know each of you and look forward to more collaborations in the future. To Ruby Peel, the unseen collaborator who pulled together five years of blog posts so I could sift through them for content, then typed references, provided feedback, and cheered me on. Thank you! I love working with you! To my friend and colleague Sara, for helping me to see that how I chose to write the book was as important as what I wrote about — and for coaching me before, during and after. To Lillie and Esther, for reading and sending feedback. It really helped! To my sister, Joanna, for helping me to find colors for the book cover that felt just right and for always believing in me. Thank you! For the team at Get It Done, who asked the right questions to help me figure out what the book was about, and then helped me get it out the door. To all the divine beings, Mother Earth, and helpers I don't yet know about, thank you for your support. And to the evergreen tree in the park — you know who you are. Thank you, too.

ABOUT THE AUTHOR/EDITOR
DEB SHINE VALENTINE, MA, PHD

From my personal experience and the experience of so many of my clients, we often find ourselves on two different sides of the spectrum: "Push" or "Puddle" (though for a few of us the puddle phase is very cleverly disguised).

Push: The place that seems to be the "norm" for us, where you're doing all the things, being nice to all the people, dismantling racism, and planning the perfect Monster-Truck themed birthday party for your 4-year-old. Fun.

Puddle: The place where you can't. For any of it. Maybe you see the warning signs and try quick fixes like that second cup of coffee, maybe you're beyond that. Depending on which side of the spectrum you're on, you're likely looking for one version of my story or another.

If you're looking for my street cred (can you say push?), here it is:

PhD in Childhood Studies, MA in Educational Ministry, BA in Elementary Education, Certified Martha Beck Life Coach, Certified Racial Justice from the Heart Facilitator, Certified

Qoya Teacher, Certified VITA™ Sex, Love, and Relationship Coach, Certified Academic Life Coach, successfully completed Tara Mohr's Playing Big Facilitator training, Future Writing®

Facilitator-in-Training, Racial Equity and Belonging consultant (in partnership with BIPOC partners). Former teacher, childcare director, executive director, and college professor.

If you're looking for evidence that I'm capable of helping you off the floor (puddle) and that I *get it*:

I know puddle well which is why my process is rooted in creating a container. A container that has endless space for all of your parts (yes, even the parts of you that you keep silent and hidden, sometimes by bribing them with ice cream). A space that feels as if it was made just for you (which it was). Just so you could get all the rest you need in this moment, all the love you need in this moment, all the nourishment you need in this moment. All the space to breathe. All of it.

Consider me like your favorite sweet and spicy chicken taco… relatable, bringing everything you need to be nourished, with just the right amount of kick that gets you to the root of what matters (because frankly, we all need a little of all of that).

And fresh guacamole, of course, or extra cheese, or both. Because always, always there must be something decadent thrown in to satisfy the hidden rebel in you.

To contact me, read my weekly blog, or learn more, visit www.thriving4equity.com.

REFERENCES

Beck, Martha. *Finding Your Way in a Wild New World: Four Steps to Fulfilling Your True Calling.* Piatkus, 1 Jan. 2012.

---. *Steering by Starlight: Find Your Right Life, No Matter What!* Rodale, 9 June 2009.

Blanco, Richard. *How to Love a Country.* Beacon Press. 26 March, 2019.

Bradford, Dr. Joy Harden (host), *Therapy for Black Girls Podcast,* (2017-present), "Therapy For Black Girls Podcast", https://therapyforblackgirls.com/podcast/

brown, adrienne maree. *Pleasure Activism: The Politics of Feeling Good.* AK Press, 13 Feb. 2019.

---. *We Will Not Cancel Us and Other Dreams of Transformative Justice.* AK Press, 17 Nov. 2020

Brown, Brené. *The Gifts of Imperfection.* Hazelden Publishing, 27 Aug. 2010.

---. *Daring Greatly: How the Courage to Be Vulnerable Transforms the Way We Live, Love, Parent, and Lead*. Penguin Books Ltd, 11 Sept. 2012.

Cameron, Julia. *The Artists Way: A Spiritual Path to Higher Creativity*. 1992. Profile Books Ltd, 4 Mar. 2022.

Cooper, Brittney. *Eloquent Rage: A Black Feminist Discovers Her Superpower*. St. Martin's Press, 20 Feb. 2019.

Davis, Angela, et al. *Abolition. Feminism. Now.* Haymarket Books, 18 Jan. 2022.

DiAngelo, Robin. *What Does It Mean to Be White? Developing White Racial Literacy*. Peter Lang, 30 May 2012.

---. *White Fragility: Why It's so Hard for White People to Talk about Racism*. Beacon Press, 26 June 2018.

Doyle, Glennon. *Untamed*. The Dial Press, 10 Mar. 2020.

Gay, Ross. *The Book of Delights*. Algonquin Books of Chapel Hill, 2019.

Hemphill, Prentis (host), *Finding Our Way*, (2020-present), https://www.findingourwaypodcast.com/

Hendricks, Gay. *The Big Leap: Conquer Your Hidden Fear and Take Life to the Next Level*. HarperCollins Publishers, 21 Apr. 2009.

Kemp, Amanda. *Say the Wrong Thing: Stories and Strategies for Racial Justice and Authentic Community*. CreateSpace, 24 Feb. 2017.

Kendi, Ibram X. *How to Be an Antiracist*. S.L., One World Publications, 13 Aug. 2019.

Kidd, Sue Monk. *The Dance of the Dissident Daughter*. Harper-Collins Publishers, 20 Aug. 2002.

Kimmerer, Robin Wall. *Braiding Sweetgrass: Indigenous Wisdom, Scientific Knowledge, and the Teachings of Plants*. Milkweed Editions, 15 Oct. 2013.

Mayer, Dr. Emeran, *The Mind-Gut Connection: How the Hidden Conversation Within Our Bodies Impacts Our Mood, Our Choices and Our Overall Health*. Harper-Wave, reprint edition, June 5, 2018.

Menakem, Resmaa. *My Grandmother's Hands: Racialized Trauma and the Pathway to Mending Our Hearts and Bodies*. Central Recovery Press, 12 Sept. 2017.

Mitchell, Sherri. *Sacred Instructions: Indigenous Wisdom for Living Spirit-Based Change*. North Atlantic Books, 13 Feb. 2018.

Mohr, Tara. *Playing Big: Find Your Voice, Your Mission, Your Message*. Penguin Random House, 29 Dec. 2015.

Nagoski, Emily. *Come as You Are: The Surprising New Science That Will Transform Your SexLife*. Simon & Schuster, 3 Mar. 2015.

Noah, Trevor. "India.Arie - Unconscious vs. Conscious Racism & Unfair Treatment of Artists" Uploaded by The Daily Show with Trevor Noah, *YouTube* 14 Feb. 2022, youtu.be/XYcn8a13Rw4. Accessed 20 Mar. 2022.

Okun, Tema. "White Supremacy Culture." *White Supremacy Culture*, 2021, www.whitesupremacyculture.info/about.html Accessed 19 Jan. 2022

Ó Tuama, Pádraig. *Daily Prayer with the Corrymeela Community*. Canterbury Press, 22 Aug. 2017.

Parker, Priya. *The Art of Gathering: How We Meet and Why It Matters*. Penguin Random House, 15 May 2018.

Pink, Daniel, *A Whole New Mind: Why Right Brainers Will Rule the World*. Penguin Publishing, March 2006.

Schieck, Rochelle. *Qoya: A Compass for Navigating an Embodied Life That Is Wise, Wild and Free*. Inspire And Move Press, 10 Jan. 2016.

Taylor, Sonya Renee. *The Body Is Not an Apology: The Power of Radical Self-Love*. Berrett-Koehler Publishers, 13 Feb. 2018.

---. *Your Body Is Not an Apology Workbook: Tools for Living Radical Self-Love*. Berrett-Koehler Publishers, 16 Mar. 2021.

Van der Kolk, Bessel. *The Body Keeps the Score: Brain, Mind and Body in the Healing of Trauma*. Penguin Books, 25 Sept. 2015.

Winters, Mary-Francis. *Inclusive Conversations*. Fostering Equity, Empathy and Belonging Across Differences. Berrett-Koehler Publishers, 2020.

Stevenson, Bryan. *Just Mercy: A Story of Justice and Redemption*. Spiegel & Grau, 18 Aug. 2015.

Tatum, Beverly Daniel. *Why Are All the Black Kids Sitting Together in the Cafeteria?* Hachette Book Group, 5 Sept. 2017.

NOTES

Introduction

1. *Google Dictionary from Oxford Languages*
2. *unitedwaynca.org*
3. *https://risetowin.org/what-we-do/educate/resource-module/equality-vs-equity/index.html*

1. Your suffering and exhaustion don't help any cause except the cause of patriarchy, white supremacy, and capitalism — even if you are White, even if you are male, and especially if you are neither White nor male

1. Cameron, Julia. *The Artist's Way: A Spiritual Path to Higher Creativity.* 1992. Profile Books Ltd, 4 Mar. 2022.

Joy is a Remedy for Injustice

1. Laverne Cox updated bell hooks' description in a tweet she sent on November 14, 2015. The original phrase, often used by bell hooks was "imperialist, white-supremacist, capitalist patriarchy." One place where you can find the phrase is in the article "Understanding Patriarchy", published by the Louisville Anarchist Federation in 2010, available online at https://imaginenoborders.org/pdf/zines/UnderstandingPatriarchy.pdf

Resources for Your Journey

1. I learned about shaking and the compost metaphor from Rochelle Schieck while training as a Qoya teacher

3. The path towards feeling better is learnable — you have the power to choose it

1. Many coaches share some version of this practice, but I first learned it from Katherine North.

4. To learn how to follow the path towards feeling better, you're going to need time, and some new guides

1. Martha Beck references various aspects of this research in *Finding Your Way in a Wild New World*, as does Daniel Pink in *A Whole New Mind: Why Right Brainers Will Rule the World* and Dr. Emeran Mayer in *The Mind-Gut Connection*. In *My Grandmother's Hands*, Resmaa Menakem discussed how ancestral trauma can be passed down in our bodies.

Resources for Your Journey

1. This practice is a simplified version of Martha Beck's Body Compass practice, combined with Body Mind mapping which I learned from her and in the VITA™ coach training program.
2. This part is adapted from some practices in the VITA™ coach training program.

5. But how will we get anything done? Pleasure as a partner to productivity

1. I learned this process in the VITA™ coach training program.

6. Alternatives to cancel culture: Boundaries, compassion, and reclaiming connection

1. Trevor Noah and India Arie had a beautiful conversation about this idea at the end of an interview on The Daily Show on Feb. 14, 2022.

Land Acknowledgments and Other Steps towards Healing and Connection with Indigenous Communities

1. https://nativegov.org/news/a-guide-to-indigenous-land-acknowl-edgment/

Resources for Your Journey

1. This was part of the VITA™ coach training program.

8. No lone wolves: If you're going to walk this path, don't go it alone

1. This idea is frequently mentioned by Progressive reformers in documents from the late 19th and early 20th centuries, when many of the current social welfare systems in the U.S. were founded. It can be seen today in continuing practices such as requiring people on food stamps to buy only certain approved items, and efforts to deny childcare to the children of mothers who are deemed to be "unworthy" of support.

Why I Believe in Affinity Groups

1. As quoted in "To Be In Rage Almost All the Time" on npr.org, June 1, 2020, 2:55 PM ET, https://www.npr.org/2020/06/01/867153918/-to-be-in-a-rage-almost-all-the-time.

Resources for Your Journey

1. *Scene on Radio* is available on Apple Podcasts and at sceneonradio.org. Topics of recent series include: Men, Seeing White, The Repair and The Land That Has Never Been Yet.